How to Be HAPPY at Work :^)

A Practical Guide to Career Satisfaction

SECOND EDITION

Arlene S. Hirsch

How to Be Happy at Work, Second Edition

Published by JIST Works, an imprint of JIST Publishing, Inc.
8902 Otis Avenue
Indianapolis, IN 46216-1033
Phone: 1-800-648-JIST Fax: 1-800-JIST-FAX E-mail: info@jist.com

Visit our Web site at **www.jist.com** for information on JIST, free job search tips, book chapters, and ordering instructions for our many products!

Quantity discounts are available for JIST books. Please call our Sales Department at 1-800-648-5478 for a free catalog and more information.

Acquisitions and Development Editor: Lori Cates Hand
Interior Designers: designLab, Seattle; Trudy Coler
Page Layout: Trudy Coler
Cover Designer: Nick Anderson
Proofreader: Deb Kincaid

Printed in Canada
07 06 05 04 03 9 8 7 6 5 4 3 2 1

Library of Congress Cataloging-in-Publication Data

Hirsch, Arlene S., 1951-

How to be happy at work : a practical guide to career satisfaction / Arlene S. Hirsch.--2nd ed.

p. cm.

Rev. ed. of: Love your work and success will follow. c1996.

Includes index.

ISBN 1-56370-980-5

1. Vocational guidance. 2. Success in business. 3. Job satisfaction. I. Hirsch, Arlene S., 1951- Love your work and success will follow. II. Title.

HF5381.H516 2004

650.1--dc22 2003017302

About This Book

It's not easy to tell others how to be happy at work, especially people who feel as if they're living in a career combat zone. I know the battleground well. For the past 20 years, I've been a career counselor, psychotherapist, and corporate outplacement consultant. In that time, I've seen more casualties of the career wars than most people experience in a lifetime. I know what it takes to be happy with your work. But I also know there's no simple formula to achieve career success and satisfaction.

The workplace is chaotic. If you're like most people, you probably feel that you're living a career nightmare: working harder to make a living with fewer available resources, more demands on your time, and lots of disincentives to achievement. Perhaps you fantasize about chucking the whole scene. Right about now, life on the golf course, ski slopes, or a sandy beach can look mighty appealing.

Maybe you just need a good, long vacation. You don't want to drop out of the workforce altogether, but you're hungering for a new adventure. You want more control over your time and your destiny. Your rallying cry is *More Freedom, Less Office Politics!*

This book is for anyone who needs a change in his or her work life. It can be a change in the kind of work you do, or in how, when, or where you do it. I'm prepared to show you how to make your career more deeply fulfilling. To use my advice, however, you'll need to set aside your normal modus operandi. I want you to open your mind to new possibilities.

Some of my ideas might seem strange initially. Please mull them over carefully before you discard them. Although my tone is, sometimes, idealistic, I'd categorize myself as a realistic optimist. You can't achieve your deepest desires without hope. And I have never met a really happy cynic.

In what many people call "the real world," it's assumed that financial success is the key ingredient to satisfaction. I question this assumption. Although economic security settles the mind and can even quiet the soul, money alone can't create deep career fulfillment. To be deeply fulfilled through work, you must integrate your financial needs and goals with your spiritual desires. I use the word "spiritual" cautiously, knowing that it's often equated with religion. What I have in mind is a more secular spirituality that doesn't call forth visions of God in the workplace. Derived from the Latin word *spiritus,* which means "breath," spirituality, in this sense, refers to those animating life principles that enable you to feel most completely alive.

When you bring energy, enthusiasm, and passion to your work, you infuse your livelihood with a vitality that drives away boredom. Add creativity, growth, meaning, and service, and you'll find that alienation will disappear, too. By adding depth to your work, you can soar to greater heights. I often see people who are successful in conventional terms but otherwise are deeply dissatisfied with their careers. If that's your situation, you might not get much sympathy from the people around you. Nevertheless, when work is not a true reflection of your interests, talents, and values, it can make you very unhappy.

In this way, I am fortunate. My counseling and writing enable me to express myself in ways that are compatible with the person I understand myself to be. They challenge me to develop my talents rather than suppress them. Although I never confuse my job title with my identity, I do believe there's a connection between your occupation and your career fulfillment. To the extent that your work enables you to develop your talents, express your beliefs, and engage your interests, it will be satisfying. Conversely, work that doesn't fit your skills and personality won't be rewarding. Therefore, if you seek career fulfillment, you must always ask yourself first and foremost: Does my work suit my needs and ambitions? If the answer is no, you must take steps to remedy that problem.

When I set out to write this book, it wasn't my intention to write a treatise on personal responsibility. But, as the project unfolded, it became abundantly clear that too much passivity is a major obstacle to career satisfaction. Far too many people live their lives according to societal, parental, or even employer agendas, instead of thinking through and acting on their own singular strengths and visions.

To see your way to a more uniquely individual life experience (and greater vocational satisfaction), you must deprogram yourself from what others want you to do and expect you to be. In writing this book, my goal is to start the ball rolling in that direction.

In part 1, I introduce a number of psychological challenges that are important to address and resolve on the road to career satisfaction, including the all-important need to create a personal life agenda and timetable.

In part 2, I address some of the tough organizational realities that have evolved over the last decade. At a time when job security has vanished and organizational restructuring is on nearly every corporate menu, it's crucial to take more aggressive responsibility for your short-and long-term career goals. Although it's difficult to control your career destiny in today's environment, which is more like emotional quicksand than solid ground, it's still possible to influence your surroundings and development in healthy ways. Amid the change and chaos, there are genuine opportunities for growth and happiness. But the spoils don't go to the timid or the passive. You have to assert yourself in the right way to the right people.

Finally, part 3 continues to pursue the theme of personal responsibility. The chapters in this part explore alternative work styles and schedules that you can adopt to increase autonomy and enhance the quality of your life; and build on the twin themes of interconnection and collaboration.

At the end of each chapter, I've included a "Thought-Starter Worksheet" to set you on the road to healthy introspection. Please don't complete these exercises on the Stairmaster. Find yourself a quiet place to reflect on your thoughts, experiences, and desires, and write your answers in the spaces provided.

We're an action-oriented society: a nation of doers. But when it comes to career fulfillment, the path to happiness begins inwardly, with introspection and self-knowledge. Professionally speaking, I was raised in the world of psychoanalysis, where there's a strongly held conviction that all healthy, self-directed action rests firmly on the foundation of self-knowledge. Knowing that, you won't be surprised to discover that my first goal in this book is to increase your capacity for introspection and deepen your self-knowledge. That process requires your active participation.

To be truly happy with your work, you must forge a path that fits your needs and life goals. No one is going to hand you the perfect career on the proverbial "silver platter." The issue, as psychiatrist Thomas Szasz tells us, is not whether or not you've found yourself; it's whether or not you've taken the time to create yourself.

Freud once identified "work" and "love" as the two greatest sources of human happiness. For me, this book has been a true labor of love. If it helps you make fulfilling life and work changes, it will have done its job and I, too, will be well satisfied.

—Arlene S. Hirsch

Dedication

To Nancy Hirsch

CONTENTS

PART 1

Career Choice and Success from Graduation to Retirement and Beyond

CHAPTER 1

Career Choice: What Do You Want to Be. . .Now That You're Grown Up?

"How old do you have to be before you feel like a grown-up in your own head?"

—Bob Greene

It was Monday morning, and my week wasn't getting off to a great start. Stuck in traffic on the Kennedy Expressway, I was already late for my first appointment with a corporate client. As I fiddled with the radio looking for a traffic report, a commercial caught my attention:

"Allison, do you want to be a ballerina when you grow up?" a man asked.

"Please, Daddy," a tiny voice replied. "I'm only three. I'm not planning to make any career decisions until I'm six."

I don't remember the product they were advertising (what could it possibly be?). But that clever two-line dialogue is permanently etched in my memory, reminding me of how much we are encouraged—and how much we encourage others—to define ourselves by our work.

Kids' fantasies often reflect their television worlds. When I was growing up, there weren't many celebrity role models for girls; and the ones that existed had helpmate or sidekick roles. There were Lois Lane,

Lucille Ball, Dale Evans, or June Cleaver from which to choose. To me, the most interesting possibilities were Annie Oakley, a hard-riding tomboy with pigtails, and Matt Dillon's worldly saloon-keeper companion, Miss Kitty.

But I didn't live in the wild, Wild West. I lived in Skokie, Illinois, where the mode of transportation was more likely to be a Chevy Impala than a horse named Bullet. Most of the women I knew really did aspire to be the suburban-perfect June Cleaver (as opposed to Barbara Billingsley, the actress who portrayed her). In those prefeminist days, real-life women who worked outside the home were routed into professions or jobs that capitalized on nurturing and caretaking roles such as nursing, teaching, social work, and secretarial jobs.

Although similarly constricted, the boys had a range of more adventurous fantasy choices. They could be Superman or Batman, the Lone Ranger or Zorro, or any one of a million athletes. My brother, who played baseball throughout grammar school, high school, and college, had dreams of being the next Mickey Mantle or Roger Maris or Willie Mays. Even their "realistic" choices looked more glamorous. Ambitious boys aspired to be doctors, lawyers, or businessmen—professions that would net them wealth, power, prestige, and recognition.

It wasn't until the sixties—when feminism and technology converged—that new dreams and possibilities opened up to and for women. Today we are just as likely to expect and want our daughters to be doctors, lawyers, and businesswomen. Young girls today still dream of becoming ballerinas or horsewomen. But they are equally enamored of becoming the next Britney Spears, Ally McBeal, or basketball star Cynthia Cooper.

Boys' fantasies haven't changed nearly as much. Young boys still dream of becoming the next superhero or superathlete. What has changed is that now they have to compete with the girls for the top spots.

Career-Choice Generation Gaps

Every generation has its collective values and beliefs. Depression-era parents passed their values for financial security, wealth, and status onto their baby-boomer children. The baby-boomer generation was the first group to collectively espouse the importance of career satisfaction along with success. When baby boomers began to discover career success was rewarding but not necessarily satisfying, they began to reexamine the values and beliefs they had internalized from their parents. They also began to pass along new messages to their own children. Interestingly, the children of baby-boomer parents are likely to complain that their parents were too open-minded or didn't provide them with enough direction.

"My parents told me that I could be anything that I wanted to be," says Leslie, a 22-year-old graduate student in psychology. "My problem is that I don't have any idea what I want to be."

Her situation is eerily reminiscent of the one that Lily Tomlin's character confronts in *The Search for Signs of Intelligent Life in the Universe* when she comments: "I always wanted to be somebody, but I should have been more specific."

When it comes to choosing your life's work—or any work at all—*you are choosing a work role, and* ***not*** *self definition.* You are not what you do. You are what you are. Your identity is comprised of your character, your values, your personality, and the many roles you play in life. You are not only a doctor or a lawyer. You are also a husband or a wife, a son or a daughter, a parent, a friend, a colleague. This is an important message to keep in mind when you want to choose or change careers.

Choosing a career often involves a journey of self-discovery. Lisa was a second-year law student when she came to me for career advice. She knew that she didn't like law or want to be a lawyer, but she worried about what other people would say if she dropped out of law school to pursue her real passion—to become a television news producer.

This was her childhood dream and her adult passion; but she worried about choosing such a competitive field.

She was facing a tough choice. Broadcast journalism is one of the most intensely competitive career choices. On the other hand, she had an undergraduate degree in journalism from a prestigious college. She was willing and able to go to graduate school in broadcast journalism to secure an educational base for her career dream. Because she was still in law school, she had not yet acquired a lavish lifestyle. She could afford to take the risk. But there was no guarantee that she would succeed.

To help her make that decision, we toyed with a larger perspective. I asked her to project herself 10 years into the future. How would she feel if she was working as a lawyer? How would she feel if she had *not* been successful in broadcast journalism?

The answers to these questions helped her get unstuck because she realized that, even if she succeeded in law, she would always question whether she could have been successful in a field she felt passionate about. Once she made a decision to take a leave of absence from law school, she was surprised at how supportive her family and friends were of her decision, and how helpful they were in connecting her up with people who worked in the television business. Although Lisa is still nervous about her future, she is so energetic and passionate about the work that others find her enthusiasm contagious. If Emerson was right that "nothing great was ever achieved without enthusiasm," she is definitely on the road to greatness.

The Hansel and Gretel Theory of Career Discovery

To uncover your career dream, my friend and colleague Cheryl Heisler recommends what she calls "the Hansel and Gretel approach." To find your way back to your original career dream, she says, you have to look for clues in the crumbs that you've abandoned along the way. Search your past for discarded interests, dreams, and goals. You might be surprised to find them still awake inside you.

Heisler knows firsthand the value of such a journey of self-discovery. Originally, she chose law because her father, a pharmacist, though it would be a good field for a bright, creative, articulate woman such as his daughter (she'd been voted "Friendliest Person" of her senior high school class). But the law isn't always the friendliest profession. It's filled with conflict and adversarial relationships. It took Heisler only a few years of practicing law to figure out that it wasn't the right choice for her.

As she looked for clues to her next career choice, she reflected back on her college major, which was advertising. She decided to pursue a position in marketing—advertising's first cousin—and subsequently landed a brand-management job at Kraft Foods.

If brand management wasn't her ultimate calling, it did prove to be a good outlet for her creativity (which made her good at positioning new products) and her outgoing personality (which made her excellent at client relationships). Along the way, she also discovered that career choice is not always a one-time experience. The more she learned about herself and the job market, the better she was able to understand how to make good choices. When she realized that product management involved too much number-crunching (for a woman who never liked math), she found herself once again on the lookout for new options.

As it turns out, she didn't have to search hard for her next career direction. Essentially, it came to her in the form of other attorneys who had heard about her career change and wanted to ask her advice on how they could change careers, too. When she discovered how much demand there was for such information and how much she enjoyed counseling other lawyers, she founded Lawternatives, a career-consulting firm that counsels lawyers about career-change options.

For Heisler, the hardest part of becoming a career counselor was giving up the job title of "lawyer." Even as a brand manager for Kraft, she referred to herself as a "lawyer who was doing marketing." She began to realize how much of her identity was vested in her job title. It was only as she grew to love her counseling business that she was able to relinquish the lawyer title.

"I have a job where I can be myself and be appreciated," says Heisler. "What better title can I wear?"

Hand-Me-Down Dreams

Cheryl Heisler looked backwards (to her career choice history) first, in order to move forward with a new dream. In addition to reclaiming a lapsed interest, she also needed to revisit her father's career advice, in order to take more personal responsibility for her choices.

Her journey reminds us that the process of self-discovery is also a separation process. You can't go forward without looking backward. You must understand how family dynamics and expectations influenced (and continued to influence) your career choices and development, in order to liberate yourself from unconscious conflicts and motivations.

This is not an indictment of your parents or your childhood. Every parent has unfulfilled dreams, wishes, and needs, which children often intuit as an unspoken demand. A father whose dream of becoming a professional baseball player was thwarted pushes his son too hard to win. A mother who regrets dropping out of law school to get married and have kids makes no secret of how gratified she is by her daughter's career decision to become a lawyer. Later, both the mother and the daughter are profoundly disappointed when the daughter finds herself temperamentally ill-suited to the profession.

In another (real-life) scenario, Richard fulfilled his father's aborted dream to become a lawyer. Richard's father had flunked out of law school in his twenties. He went into the construction business and the bar business, and ultimately owned a restaurant. But Richard's father never forgot his first dream.

When Richard, his firstborn son, decided to go to law school to become a lawyer, his father was thrilled with his son's decision and forever after lived vicariously through his son's many career achievements. Fortunately, Richard liked and was well-suited to the law. This was not true for his younger brother, David, an equally talented and ambitious young man who made a name for himself in the field of medicine. Despite David's equally impressive career achievements, his father never showed the same interest or pride in David's career. His dad simply couldn't relate to his son's ambitions or accomplishments.

As kids, we use our parents like mirrors. We solicit their advice, observe their choices, and respond to their expectations. It can take a lifetime to realize that your parents' advice might have been bad advice (or, at least, bad for you). Part of growing up is recognizing that your parents don't have all the answers. To find your way to a more fulfilling work life, you might have to *unlearn* some of that flawed advice you got from your mom and dad.

Eleanor Roosevelt was right when she said, "You can't live anyone else's life—not even your child's." Why, then, do so many parents feel compelled to present their kids with ready-made answers to Life's Tough Questions rather than help them develop the experience, self-knowledge, and self-confidence to create their own solutions? Although parents do have a responsibility to instill good values, much of what parades as the "right thing to do" can relate more to parental narcissism than any objective standard of correctness. Too many parents push their own personal dream of success and call it reality.

Lauren was a 28-year-old accountant who came to see me because she was bored to tears by her career and wanted to do something more creative. A closer examination of her career history revealed that she had chosen accounting because her accountant-father told her it was a "good profession." She trusted his wisdom and followed his advice, only to discover that it was all wrong for her.

When she went back to her father to ask him why he thought accounting was a good profession when she found it so boring, he replied: "I said it was a good profession. I never said it was interesting."

Too late, Lauren realized her mistake. When she said she wanted a good profession, she meant that she wanted an *interesting* profession. Her father was working with a different mindset. To him, a good profession was one where he could make a lot of money and support his family's lifestyle. Once she realized her own needs for more interesting and creative work, Lauren went back to school and became an interior designer, a field which she finds more creatively stimulating.

My career counseling practice is filled with stories like this: young men and women who followed their parents' career advice, only to discover that it made them unhappy. Much of the time, the parents assumed that a well-paying job would make their kids happy. What their offspring are discovering is that "making money" is a necessary condition for career success and satisfaction; but it is not sufficient. You need to make money at work that is meaningful to you.

When I was growing up, my parents shared a dream for my brother to become either an accountant or a tax attorney. This reflected their Depression-era dreams for financial stability and comfort. My brother's needs and dreams were different. He valued creativity and intellect above all else, which is why he chose to become a writer and an English professor. My parents worried obsessively that he would "starve." But they underestimated their son's intellectual talents, as well as his enormous competitive drive to succeed. Had he followed their advice and become a tax attorney, he would undoubtedly have failed miserably for several reasons. He is not skilled in mathematics; he has no interest in tax or law; making money is important to him, but it has never been his first priority. He would have found the work and the environment intellectually and creatively boring. His passion for his work—and particularly his love of literature and poetry—has fueled much of his success.

There Are No Perfect Career Choices

There is no one right answer to the question "what do you want to be when you grow up?" Nor is there any cookie-cutter formula for success. Good choices are individual choices. They are based on an understanding of how to interweave your individual interests, abilities, values, and personality with the job market. Some of the best career paths are ones that you create for yourself based on your talents and the world's needs.

Part of growing up, it seems, means figuring out that your parents don't have all the answers, even if they think they do. In a wonderful episode from *The Wonder Years,* the television series about a baby boomer nostalgically reliving his years of innocence, 12-year-old Kevin Arnold goes to work with his normally gruff and unapproachable father one day. The encounter turns into an important "coming-of-age" experience.

Dressed in matching suits and ties, the two male Arnolds are greeted by a small staff of fawning employees who pinch Kevin's cheeks and ask him what he wants to be when he grows up. Inside his father's office, Kevin is astounded and impressed by the "grown-up toys" he sees everywhere—but especially his father's Big Desk and Giant Chair.

His father is immediately bombarded with emergency phone calls and people crises. As he adroitly handles them one by one, Kevin leans back in the Giant Chair and props his feet up on the Big Desk, watching the action and fantasizing about "how great it must be to have power."

A rare moment of father-son intimacy ensues a few minutes later when, in the cafeteria, Kevin asks his father: "Did you always want to be the Manager of Distribution Support and Product Services?" His father laughs, telling his son, "When I was your age, I wanted to be captain of a big ship with a big mast. Be on the ocean. Navigate by the stars."

When asked about what happened to his dream, Mr. Arnold describes how he generally settled into adult responsibilities. He claims no regret about the lost dreams of youth. "You can't do every silly thing you want in life," he tells his son. Back at the office, Kevin's dad is accosted by his boss and chewed out for not taking his phone calls. As Kevin looks on, the Big Boss threatens to fire his father if he ever makes that mistake again. Mr. Arnold never says a word in his own defense.

Later that night, father and son stand outside gazing upward at the stars, pondering the day's events. As his father searches the sky for Polaris, Kevin realizes that he, too, has lost something. His father doesn't scare him anymore.

I wish that my client "Claudia" had learned that same lesson before she relinquished her childhood dream of becoming a "singer, actress, or teacher" to follow her father's dictate that she go to medical school and become a doctor. Her father, who was a health-care administrator, always wanted to be a doctor. But, as a (pre–civil rights) African-American male, he encountered too much racial discrimination to pursue his dream. He was determined that his children would have the advantages and rights that he had never had.

By her own admission, Claudia never had the courage to defy her father; but she never wanted to be a doctor, either. She assumed that he knew best and now, at 35 years old, she is paying the price for that misguided belief. "I'm living my father's dream," she says, "and it's making me miserable."

The real problem with parents who foist their personal preferences onto their children isn't so much whether the parent is right or wrong, but that the parent is taking over a decision that isn't theirs to make. As a child, you might not feel free to choose; but as an adult, you are.

The road to adulthood is paved with renunciation. But whether that renunciation takes the form of giving up your personal dream (as Kevin's father did), or giving up the belief that your parents are omniscient and omnipotent (as Kevin did), is up to you. What is clear is that, as an adult, you have a responsibility to forge your own reality and make your own choices. It's up to you how much you want to risk and how much you want to compromise.

To this day, Claudia regrets that she did not pursue her dream of becoming a singer. Although she knows that it would have been risky, she also wonders whether she could have been successful at it, if she had focused all of her energy and attention on that goal. With so many student loans to repay, she feels increasingly trapped by her financial responsibilities, even though she makes a good living as a physician.

What many people (of all ages) fail to realize is how important it is to like and care about the work you do—to do work you love and love the work you do. Tom Peters, a noted author and management consultant, has said that when it comes to career choices, it's inconceivable to him that ambitious and talented people would do anything other than follow their hearts toward things they love. How can you possibly expect to be successful, Peters asks, if you don't care about and value the work you do?

Looking Forward to Career Growth

The Hansel and Gretel strategy requires some 20/20 hindsight. It involves learning from your mistakes and redirecting your path toward more rewarding and fulfilling choices. But there is also a part of you that needs to go exploring, to learn about career fields and choices to which you might not yet have gained exposure.

There might be 26,000 occupations in the labor force, but most people tend to focus their attention on a handful of possibilities. Rather than limit yourself to specific job titles (which can often be misleading), try focusing on what career consultant Bernard Haldane called "motivated skills." A motivated skill is something that you like to do, and do well. That's how an insurance claims manager who likes project management and writing became a technical writer, a CPA with a passion for New Age health care became a spa manager, and a systems engineer with an innate talent for foreign languages positioned herself as an international expert in telecommunications. Instead of focusing on job titles, these successful career changers did some "soul-searching" to figure out what they were really good at and loved to do. Then they positioned themselves accordingly.

There are also career changers whose primary motivation is to keep on growing and learning. What they want is variety, challenge, and intellectual stimulation. These are people who should expect to change careers voluntarily several times over the course of their working lives because they will always need a new challenge. To become too closely identified with a job title or career identity would be severely self-limiting.

This is how (and why) a test engineer became an engineering manager, a management consultant, an entrepreneur, and finally, a professor. At each transition point in his career path, he determined what he needed to do in order to stay stimulated and energized—and then committed himself to doing it.

Changing Careers—The New Norm

The days of choosing one career for life are long gone. Perhaps they should never have existed at all. Isn't it unrealistic to think that the career choice you made at 20 should automatically suit your needs at 30, 40, 50, or 60? If your first career choice doesn't work out the way you once hoped it would, there's no reason why you can't continue to make new choices that better suit your needs. My oldest career-change client was age 70 when she decided to retire from medicine and pursue a law degree. (She then became a medical-legal consultant to a medical products manufacturer.)

Somewhere along the line you might have picked up the mistaken idea that the need for growth stops in adulthood. But it is only people with limited career ambitions or those who "learned everything they needed to know in kindergarten" who can expect to roll gracefully into retirement without changing one iota.

To lead a fulfilling life, you need to keep challenging yourself to grow at every stage in your life. Frank Mackey exemplifies that philosophy. Mackey retired from a successful law practice in Little Rock, Arkansas, (in his sixties) to pursue an acting career in Chicago. Later he moved on to New York City. This isn't his first career change. His previous vocational hats include sales, marketing, human resources, and business management. He also preaches what he practices. One of the most liberating career moments for Mackey's son came with his father's recommendation that he "stop trying to choose for life and start thinking in five-year increments." From that day forward, the younger Mackey felt free to pursue careers on the stock exchange, in business management, and in real estate.

Many baby-boomer parents have been reluctant to make the same mistakes that their parents did. When it comes to offering career advice and guidance, they are inclined to tell their sons and daughters that "you can do anything you want to do." Although their kids often appreciate all this freedom of choice, they also often complain that the advice is unhelpful.

"I know I can do anything I want to do," says Leslie, a 21-year-old retail sales clerk. "My problem is I don't know what I want to do." Nor can she be expected to. She hasn't worked long enough or developed strong enough vocational interests to be able to make a good career choice. What she needs to do is to commit herself to the process of figuring out what career choice makes the most sense for her. Leslie can follow her interests and experiment with new skills and different environments. Her goal should be to learn more about herself and the job market, and to gain more confidence in her abilities (and more skills). In her case, a career plan is nothing more—or less—than a highly individualized learning plan. She needs to focus on identifying what she needs to know and learn in order to make good career decisions.

This advice doesn't just apply to 20-year-olds. If you've been working in one career field or industry for any length of time, you might not know enough about other career opportunities or feel qualified enough to pursue other options. Recognizing your limitations does not have to be the endpoint. It should become the starting point for new growth and development.

Becoming a Grown-Up

Gerontologist Stephen Baum makes the distinction between cultural adulthood and emotional adulthood. *Cultural adults* are people who have acquired the possessions of adulthood. They have houses, cars, and kids. They live adult lives. *Emotional adulthood* has different requirements. Emotional adulthood means making authentic choices and living an authentic life.

When columnist Bob Greene asked, "How old are you supposed to be before you become a grown-up in your own head?" he was reflecting on the consequences that come from living your life according to someone else's agenda. Taking on the conventions of adulthood might make you a cultural adult; but it can also keep you one step removed from your real dreams and desires.

Author Tom Clancy remembers the moment when he reached that epiphany. He was in his mid-thirties at the time, living the traditional American dream. He had a wife, two kids, and a fairly successful career in the insurance business. He also had a car and car payments, a house with a mortgage, and other trappings of middle-class respectability. But he knew something was missing when he asked himself for the umpteenth time: "What do I want to be when I grow up?"

Says Clancy: "The stunning and depressing realization hit me that I was grown up, and I might not be what I wanted to be."

Clancy's dilemma reflects a failure of imagination. What he lacked was a dream of his own. He was so busy following society's agenda, he hadn't realized that he was programming himself for unhappiness. The type of success he had been taught would make him content turned out to be surprisingly unfulfilling.

To arrive at a more emotionally satisfying resolution, he had to make more self-directed choices, to forge a different kind of connection to his work that would enable him to express himself more fully. Clancy was an insurance broker with a passion for naval history. He had once dreamed of writing a novel that reflected that passion. So, he handed over the reins of his insurance business to his wife while he wrote a novel about a Russian submarine captain who defects, along with his submarine, to the United States. *The Hunt for Red October* was the first of many Tom Clancy successes and the beginning of a new literary genre known as the techno-thriller that includes *Red Rabbit, Shadow Warriors, The Bear and the Dragon,* and *Patriot Games.*

Many dissatisfied careerists recognize themselves in Clancy's dilemma. Surrounded with financial responsibilities, it isn't easy to "follow your dream"—or even to find it under all the layers of conventional thinking that obscure it.

Can Money Buy Happiness?

Money plays an important role in career choice and development. But it does not play the same role for everyone. How much money you need to make depends on: (1) your financial goals; and (2) your personal values. If you are not a money-oriented kind of person, it simply doesn't make sense to choose a career strictly for its financial rewards. It is unrealistic to think that you will be able to stay motivated in a career or profession that is meaningless to you. More likely you will end up feeling trapped by what career experts call "golden handcuffs." People with golden handcuffs are chained to their jobs or professions either because they can't afford to leave or because they have become so attached to the financial rewards that they don't want to make less money, even though they hate their work.

This is definitely the case for my friend Joel. Joel is a lawyer who has worked in the same office for 20 years. He can do the work with his eyes closed; and, in fact, he often does, which accounts for why he feels like he's sleepwalking through the day. Joel claims he wants to change careers—"to do something meaningful and important." But he's been waffling for years because he doesn't want to give up his safe job and comfortable income. Although this is definitely understandable, he is also digging a vocational grave for himself. The longer he waits, the harder the change will become. At 45, he doesn't have an infinite amount of time left to work. If he doesn't make a move soon, he might not be able to make a move at all. Joel never had a specific career passion. Early in his career, he wanted to be a professional, make some money, and feel secure. After 20-plus years following that gold-brick road, he now wants to do something that is more meaningful to him.

The initial emphasis that parents and their offspring place on money is quite reasonable. As a young adult, you are cast from the family womb without an apartment or a job or much of a bank account to sustain you. One important goal of young adulthood is to establish financial independence. Plus, society has another timetable in store for you. Aspiring professionals expect to graduate from college, get a job, get married, buy a house, and have kids.

And after "have kids"? Raise kids. Pay the bills. Save for college tuition. After that, your kids can do the same thing all over again: live your life, that is.

It's all very predictable. It's also unrealistic.

Every individual has to make his or her own way in the world. There's no cookie-cutter formula that works for everyone. Behind every successful careerist is a process of self-discovery and a journey down a personally meaningful road, not a simple prescription for happiness that didn't work then and doesn't work now.

Take a Personal Career Interest Survey

Most people don't know enough about all their available options to make informed career decisions. To remedy that deficit, you'll need to do some market research:

1. Start by making a general list of your personal and professional interests. Don't omit any options because of preconceived notions about a field or industry.
2. Write down your number one interest and then consider it carefully. What is it about that area that most fascinates you? For

example, a woman who loves cooking realized she's particularly drawn to desserts because they appeal to both her sense of artistry and her sweet tooth.

3. Explore your interest more deeply, by researching the following:
   - Companies that produce related products or services
   - Schools that teach related skills
   - Types of jobs related to your interest
   - Names of specific people who work in the field
4. Set up an action plan—complete with realistic goals and timetables—to meet (or at least talk on the phone with) people who work in your targeted interest area. In your discussions, try to learn as much as possible about what these professionals are doing. Also ask for referrals to people working in related fields. After each meeting, take careful notes to consolidate your learning; then set new exploration goals.
5. When you've completed your research, listen to your gut. Does pursuing your targeted field still seem to be an exciting idea? If so, figure out what steps you'll have to take to become a qualified candidate in that field.
6. If your answer is a more cautious "maybe," determine what else you need to know to make an informed career decision. Then, make it your goal to get that data.
7. If you decide that your top interest doesn't translate into viable career options, return to your list to determine your second, third, and even fourth choices. Then repeat the exploratory process until you find a promising direction.
8. If you're still undecided after several rounds of this process, think more creatively about ways to combine your interests. The prospective pastry chef, for example, had a seemingly conflicting interest in weight management. By tying together her two interests, she developed a specialty in low-fat desserts.

If you're like many people, you might discover a latent desire to paint or write or act. You might want to build something beautiful, make a different contribution to our world, or perhaps leave an inspirational legacy. Let your imagination roam wild. You might be surprised at what you discover.

Many people who do this exercise find that they want to add something of value to the world. One wanted to build a golf course in the inner city. Another wanted to create a foundation to promote good works.

Others go for adventure and travel. In their imaginations, they became tour guides to the Orient, Middle East, or Africa. Or, combining adventure and service, they consider becoming a missionary in Peru, a public-health nurse in West Africa, or a teacher in Bosnia.

Freedom ranked high on the list of desires. Very few people expressed a desire to work for someone else, although many were interested in public service. Almost no one continued in the same line of work. Muriel and John James, the mother-son team who wrote *Passion For Life* (1991, Penguin Books), call these desires "a hunger of the soul searching for more."

However liberating it would be, most of us will never clean up in the lottery. Still, I wonder if it's really necessary, financial considerations notwithstanding, to live so far from the heart of your desires; to put moneymaking above all other needs and goals; to abandon the things you love and care about to make a living.

Hearkening back to Cheryl Heisler's story, her experimentation with a variety of work roles and her willingness to learn from each experience enabled her to make a unique and meaningful career choice. To do the same, you might have to move beyond the things your parents wanted for you (and needed from you).

Self-knowledge can be elusive. But more than any objective inventory of skills and interests, the ability to learn from experience is the key to self-knowledge. Putting a modern-day spin on Plato's famous statement "The unexamined life is not worth living," management theorist Warren Bennis says, "The unexamined life is impossible to live successfully."

Perhaps it's time to stop measuring success by external standards of performance and start measuring it in more qualitative terms—specifically, by your level of satisfaction and fulfillment. Time's a-wastin'. So why not use it wisely? Take some chances on your own happiness. It might almost make you feel like a kid again.

Career Choice: What Do You Want to Be... Now That You're Grown Up? Thought-Starter Worksheet

1. Do you remember having a first career dream? If so, what was it?

runner

2. How did your parents respond to your dream?

discouraging

3. How did you feel about your parents' response?

let down, [illegible] off

4. Did your parents have a career ambition for you? If so, what was it?

No. A teacher?

(continues)

(continued)

5. How did you feel about your parents' career dream for you?

Didn't want to be a teacher

6. Do you feel that your parents' career guidance was based on a good understanding of your skills and interests?

?

7. Do you feel that your parents' career guidance was based on a good understanding of the job market?

?

8. Did your parents have careers? If so, what were they?

NO.

9. If your parents had careers, do you feel that they were satisfied with their own choices?

NO

10. Can you identify any way in which your parents' career choices influenced the choices they encouraged you to make?

No.

11. If your parents were raised during the Depression, do you think that experience influenced their career advice to you? If so, how?

Yes. Be practical

12. Did you follow your parents' career recommendation? Why or why not?

Yes. It just sort of happened

13. If you followed your parents' recommendation, how do you feel about your choice now?

I could have done better

14. If you could make your career choice all over again, what would you do differently?

Done my MA in painting; taken art more seriously

CHAPTER 2

Do You Know the Secrets of Career Success?

Nothing will ever be attempted, if all possible objections must be first overcome.

—Samuel Johnson

Times change. People change. Technology progresses and challenges everyone to adapt to new ways of living and working. Suddenly, the phrase "24/7" has entered the collective psyche. Like convenience grocery stores, everyone is suddenly "on-call." The corrugated carton salesman carries a pager. Employees interrupt their personal therapy sessions to respond to phone calls from the office. The woman standing in front of you at Starbucks holds up the line while she converses with her secretary and her nanny. Your date takes an order from his customer on his cell phone while you peruse the wine list. Even on vacation, you can't help but overhear other people's business or escape gluing yourself to your laptop computer lest you miss some urgent communication.

Yes, the world has gone crazy. In the blink of a workplace eyelash, the Internet economy mushroomed exponentially and then crashed. Everywhere we looked there were new young multimillionaires. Blink twice and you're looking at a whole new generation of cynics and paupers.

One day the economy is growing; and seemingly overnight the experts are predicting (and hunkering down for) a recession. Blink again and the United States has gone to war. Patriotism is the new American religion; firefighters, the new American heroes.

Everywhere you go, you are bombarded with new information and developments. As things continue to spin out of control, it can be so hard to feel like you are still the captain of your own ship, the master of your own fate.

The Gold Rush mentality that ushered in the "dot-com" economy left many people hungering to make their first million by the age of 25 and then retire to a life of fun and play. So, why didn't Bill Gates, the billionaire founder of Microsoft, retire along with them? We can only assume that he is in the game for more than money. The truth is that Gates likes the game. He likes to challenge himself and his people to change the world. One of the most amazing things this "Pope of PC" ever said is that he believes "Success is a lousy teacher. It seduces smart people into thinking they can't lose."

This chapter is a reminder that, no matter how much the world changes (and your life changes with it), there are still some timeless truths about what it takes to be successful: truths that make as much sense today as they did 100 years ago.

Rule 1: Motivation Is the Key to Success

"It's not that I'm so smart, it's just that I stay with problems longer."

—Albert Einstein

Knowing your own motivational triggers is an important key to developing and sustaining a successful career. Some people are motivated to make a lot of money. I remember working, for example, with a stockbroker who was discontent with his $200,000-a-year income. To him, the dollars represented a scorecard. A man who made "only" $200,000 a year in financial services did not—in his estimation—qualify as an unmitigated success. To be truly successful, he wanted and needed to take more risks, which is why he ultimately ended up in the venture-capital business. To achieve that goal, however, he needed to have more confidence in his own abilities and judgment and more determination to pursue a riskier career path. Because he had a family (and a somewhat extravagant lifestyle) to support, he needed to do some real soul-searching before he cavalierly put that lifestyle at risk.

What he learned about himself from our counseling conversations is that he would never, ever jeopardize his family's financial well-being. He would do everything in his power to ensure their financial security, including minimizing some of the risks he might otherwise take if he did not have a wife and a family to support. His motivation to make more money without putting his family at risk were dual motivating factors for him, which helped him make prudent investment decisions based on a solid appreciation of his own "risk tolerance."

The Motivation of Money

Money is often an important motivating factor. But money doesn't mean the same thing to everyone, nor does everyone have the same financial needs. For some people, money represents success. Others view it as a form of security. It can also provide a measure of autonomy, independence, and peace of mind. Or it can be a burden. For Claudia (the doctor who wanted to be a singer, who we discussed in chapter 1), the pursuit of money as a symbol of success was actually demotivating. Had she known herself better—and had the courage to stand up to her father—she would have chosen a career that was more intellectually and artistically stimulating. Although she appreciated (and still appreciates) the "value of a dollar," she is more motivated to earn her dollars in positions that do not involve direct service. She simply finds the caretaking tasks of medicine too draining.

Know What Motivates You

The key to understanding personal motivation is in knowing what energizes you—what kinds of activities, people, places, and situations are personally stimulating and fulfilling? For John, a systems analyst, teamwork and a spirit of innovation are the keys to sustaining motivation. John has a tendency to change careers every three or four years because he outgrows his environment. When he begins to feel like he knows more than his boss and any of his colleagues or that the environment is resistant to change, he grows bored and needs to move on. After each job change, he finds himself reenergized by a new set of challenges and teammates. However, we have never been able to identify an environment that is socially and creatively stimulating enough to last longer. What John and I now understand about him is that he is not the kind of professional who is destined to start and end his career in a safe place. He likes his financial security. But his security does not depend on continuous employment with a single employer. His "nest egg" is something that he is building on his own, through dint of hard work and investment savvy.

Sally is motivated by the need to make a contribution. She needs to feel like her work matters and makes a difference. This need convinced Sally to switch from banking to fundraising. Both professions involve a "bottom-line" mentality; however, Sally enjoys the challenge of using her ingenuity and people skills to raise funds for worthy causes. In banking, she often felt like a cog in the wheel of commerce, rather than a real contributor.

Rule 2: Success Takes Hard Work

"I'm blown away by your ability to show up."

That's what Keanu Reeves' character Conor O'Neill in the movie "Hard Ball" tells his ballplayers when, despite enormous odds, they make their way to the championship game. Of course, Hollywood thrives on these kinds of uplifting fantasies. The power of a dream coupled with determination and hard work turns out to be their particular formula for success.

Thomas Edison once remarked that "a genius is a talented person who does his homework." He also wisely remarked that good fortune tends to favor the prepared. Henry Ford echoed that sentiment when he remarked, "Before everything else, getting ready is the secret of success."

Any meteoric rise to success takes preparation and hard work. Bill Gates was a computer geek before he was catapulted into the world limelight. Michael Jordan was a hard-working and determined high school and college athlete before he became one of the greatest superstar athletes of all time. Yes, these are very rich men. They are also men who devoted themselves to their work, who were willing to work hard, and who are not afraid of setbacks and failures. They know that success depends on the ability to learn from mistakes, overcome challenges, and keep on keepin' on.

Ambition Alone Isn't Enough

It is not enough to be ambitious. The world is filled with ambition. But the path to success is littered with discarded dreams and disillusioned people who never achieved the recognition or success they felt they deserved. Is it because there's isn't enough room for everyone to be King or Queen of the Mountain? Or is it because people waste so much time and energy climbing the wrong mountain?

It's natural to want to be a success. And it can be gratifying to find yourself on the fast track. But the knowledge that you were promoted often in your career is seldom enough to sustain you over the long haul—especially when the express lanes to the top get clogged with competition.

Sure, it would be great if you could just leapfrog over the people in front of you; if you could skip having to make investments of time, energy, and money in skill-and-credential-building and go straight to the rewards. As Jack Kerouac once said, though, "Walking on water wasn't built in a day." There's a learning curve. Also, the lessons and skills you learn on the path to accomplishment might be every bit as rewarding as the end goal.

Celebrating Everyday Successes

Indeed, it's wiser to think in terms of "everyday successes" or little wins, rather than focus on some giant jackpot. Little wins eventually add up to big wins and are much more easily achievable. They include the satisfaction of resolving a customer dispute, gaining a new skill, writing a report, getting a good performance appraisal, improving on an existing ability, and learning to handle constructive criticism. These little victories can make the difference between a good day and a bad one. They are also the building blocks of a good reputation, the name you acquire for yourself through your work.

Rule 3: Follow Your Dream

Missions are the values or dreams that drive superachievers to pursue excellence. To fly higher than that, you also need to dig a little deeper. When clinical psychologist Charles Garfield first researched superachievers in business, he wanted to know what made them different. In his book *Peak Performers,* Garfield reveals the secret that enables these executives to achieve consistently impressive and satisfying results without burning out. Says Garfield: "The bottom line for peak performers is that they went and pursued their dreams." Why? Because dreamers who are committed to making their visions come true often keep a close eye on anything and anyone that might interfere with their ability to bring the dream to life. Their intense ambition can make them incredibly pragmatic when it comes to achieving their goals.

What's in a Mission?

If the notion of a "mission" at first sounds too religious or impractical, think again. For your work to be meaningful, you must have a vocational mission that reflects and expresses your spirituality.

Like the urge of plants to grow toward sun and water, human beings have an overarching need for growth that's expressed through a variety of spiritual urges. In *Passion for Life* (1991, Penguin Books), authors Muriel and John James outline a simple yet elegant framework that should help you determine whether spiritual components are missing from your work. Formulate your mission accordingly:

- **The urge to live** involves basic survival needs and more. It's expressed through your desire to be as healthy as possible.
- **The urge to be free**—physically, emotionally, and intellectually—is another fundamental force within the human spirit. But it takes courage to stand up for your freedom and live in accordance with your personal needs and beliefs.
- **The urge to understand** is also universal. It makes you search for knowledge that can give you greater control over your environment and your life. When you don't understand the factors that affect your life, you tend to feel helpless and confused.
- **The urge to create** activates unique ways of thinking, being, and doing through goals that express your originality. If you lack creative outlets, you can become angry, indifferent, or unproductive.
- **The urge to enjoy** is as natural as the urge to live. It can push you to search for happiness and pleasure in everyday things. When you bring a playful spirit to your activities, what you do feels less important than how you do it.
- **The urge to connect** creates a genuine bond of caring with others. It's one of the motivations behind a strong desire to serve.
- **The urge to transcend** is defined as the ability to reach up and out—to move beyond the ordinary limitations of human existence. It's a fundamental component of nearly every religious system and many religious impulses.

At the heart of every peak performer, Garfield found a desire to excel at something the person truly cared about. In these achievers, economic self-interest combined with other, more spiritual values involving creativity and service. These values became leverage points for excellence.

Mission-Driven Career Change

A lot of mission-driven career changers emerged after the collapse of the World Trade Center on 9/11. In the face of so much individual heroism and tragedy, many ambitious and talented men and women suddenly felt compelled toward more meaningful work. For example, inquiries about joining the Peace Corps spiked 20 percent in the two months following the tragedy. Others switched from for-profit employers to nonprofit organizations in an effort to create more meaningful, service-oriented work lives.

No generation has been more affected by this tragedy than people in their twenties and thirties. Suddenly Gen-Xers are being transformed into "Generation 911" in the same way baby boomers were affected by Vietnam and the generation before them was shaped by World War II and the Depression. This is what prompted "Sam," a 29-year-old real-estate broker, to ditch his real-estate career to go back to school to become a social worker. This is also what prompted Katie, a college junior, to take a year off from her studies in order to do some volunteer work. And it's what motivated Simon, a 25-year-old teacher, to become a police officer.

These career-change stories are both heartwarming and surprisingly predictable. Tragedy often becomes the impetus for positive personal changes. Take, for example, John Walsh, the popular television host of "America's Most Wanted." Walsh became a crusader for justice after his six-year-old son, Adam, was abducted and killed. Similarly, the inspiration for MADD (Mothers Against Drunk Driving) came from Candy Lightner when her teenage daughter, Cari, was killed by a drunk driver.

Discovering Your Passion

Sometimes, as an adult, it's hard to discover a dream or a mission. Other times, the difficulty is in recognizing it when you've found it. To discover your passion, you must ask yourself what you place at the center of your life—what you personally find most fulfilling. Then, build your livelihood around that central interest or value.

Rules for Creating a "Burning-with-Passion" Work Life

1. Choose work you love.
2. Commit to competence.
3. Invest in training.
4. Chart a course of action.
5. Set goals.
6. Cultivate a problem-solving mentality.
7. Build and nurture support systems.
8. Monitor your progress.
9. Rechart your course when necessary to take advantage of new experiences and learning.
10. Keep setting new goals—and keep on truckin'.

Begin by looking at the position you currently hold. Are you happy where you are? Being discontented doesn't necessarily indicate the need to change careers entirely. You might simply need to redirect your career toward more personally fulfilling goals.

For example, a 40-year-old pharmacologist in Chicago had devoted 20 years to academic research on psychogenic drugs. On the surface, if looked like he enjoyed a satisfying and challenging academic career. As the principal investigator on several research grants, he enjoyed senior status and had accumulated an impressive list of research publications. Yet he actually viewed his projects as "assembly-line research."

"After awhile I was just plugging new drugs into the same experimental design" he explains. "There was nothing new or challenging about it. It was boring."

Beating Career Boredom

Boredom is an important symptom of career distress. Regardless of where you fit in the organizational hierarchy, it can mean that you are underemployed: You simply have more skills and abilities than your job requires. Boredom, in my experience, is one of the number-one reasons why adults change careers. It is an expression of unused potential. Eventually, the pharmacologist grew so frustrated with his situation that he quit. He gave himself a year of play to reconnect with the things he loved to do because he'd given up many of his "fun" interests early in life to concentrate on earning a Ph.D. and building an academic career. In that year of leisure, he discovered that science was still his core interest. However, he needed to apply his skills in a broader and more personally meaningful context, perhaps in consumer research or education.

His career story is a reminder that professional plateaus represent ideal opportunities to reexamine your needs and values and, if necessary, redirect your career into arenas that stimulate new growth. It is not enough to look backward; you might also need to look forward, to learn more about the options that are available to you, in order to discover your own personal career dream.

Rule 4: Honor Your Talents

When Harvard psychologist Howard Gardner conducted his landmark research on multiple intelligences, he opened the door to a fuller understanding of human potential. Gardner has become an advocate for educational reform and a pioneer in the research of human potential, criticizing our society's traditional emphasis on verbal and analytical abilities as the pinnacle of intelligence. In their stead, he has put forth a more expanded vision that includes linguistic, musical, spatial, kinesthetic, emotional, interpersonal, and intrapersonal intelligences. The more we, as individuals, are able to develop our many intelligences, the more capable and evolved we will become. Understanding yourself as a multifaceted individual with many talents and possibilities also enables you to expand your vision of your own career potential.

Balancing Creative Urges with a Need for Income

In another life, my friend Chel was a real-estate financier with verbal, mathematical, and interpersonal skills. She worked hard to acquire an MBA from a prestigious university and built a successful career in business. But what she really hungered to do was to develop her creativity—to write and to paint. After her kids were grown and she had moved in with her boyfriend, she had the opportunity to devote herself to developing those skills. Although she hopes to someday be able to support herself through her writing, she knows that there can be a long incubation period, and that writing is a skill and a talent that takes enormous amounts of time and commitment. It is not a process that can be rushed.

At 25, Jeremy is at a crossroads in his life. He is a dedicated musician who writes songs and plays music with a band. He would like to make music a full-time career. But he hasn't been able to make enough money. So, he works days as a customer-service representative. After five years in this entry-level position, he realizes that he needs to develop another talent if he wants any kind of satisfying day job. Because he is good with his hands, loves to build and fix things, and enjoys computers, he decided to educate himself to become a software engineer. By developing several of his different "intelligences," Jeremy has been able to piece together a life that includes a successful day job and a passion for making music.

Develop Your Full Potential

Many ambitious people underestimate their own potential or fail to invest themselves fully in their own talents. When you commit yourself to developing your full potential, you will undoubtedly enjoy the career-building process more because you will not be focusing exclusively on external rewards. The process of growing and developing the range of your abilities can be inherently satisfying. It also affords you the opportunity to combine your talents in creatively interesting ways that enable you to create a unique career path for yourself.

No one is better at this than my brother—the poet, Edward Hirsch. As a successful poet, Eddie has obviously developed his love of language and his linguistic abilities to their fullest potential. But there is another side to him that accounts equally for his enormous success. He excels in what Gardner calls the "personal intelligences." According to Gardner, there are two personal intelligences. The first one is *intrapersonal.* It involves self-knowledge, particularly the knowledge and management of your own emotions. Reading my brother's poetry, I can't help but notice how well he describes and captures complex feelings and emotional states. The second personal intelligence is *interpersonal* intelligence. This is my brother's second enormous gift. He is an inspiring and charismatic teacher whose students would gladly follow him to the proverbial "far ends of the earth." He invests himself wholeheartedly in developing their intellectual and artistic talents and is known for his enormous generosity to other writers. Not only has he developed these talents fully, he also is one of the most passionate, committed, and hardworking men I have ever met. He is living proof that talent, passion, and a lot of hard work can create the miracle of genius.

Rule 5: Manage Yourself

There's no direct correlation between success and mental health. We all know that you can be an "S.O.B." and still be successful. You *can* win the rat race and still be a rat. But if you manage yourself well, you can also win the rat race without *turning into* a rat. This involves developing a good working relationship among your thoughts, feelings, and actions. In the "real world" of work, you don't get punished for having bad thoughts. You can think the meanest, nastiest things in the world as long as you don't lose your temper and act on them. Anger, like all strong feelings, must be managed productively.

Standing Up for Yourself

"Selene" prizes the fact that she is a team player. She is also a 50-year-old woman who has worked very hard to achieve success in the male-dominated world of engineering. She values her ability to be a leader and to mentor the people on her team so that they develop their talents. What comes harder to her is the ability to assert herself and her authority. She's been known to crumble in the face of direct competition.

Selene learned how to mend the error of her ways when one of her much younger colleagues began shamelessly stealing her work. First, this young woman erased Selene's name from a report and then distributed the report under her own name. She tried to convince her boss to kick Selene off an international committee so that she could participate instead...etc., etc., etc.

Selene's first impulse was to wring this young woman's neck. Her second impulse was to cry. And her third impulse was to bury her head in shame. Fortunately, her next impulse was to call her career counselor so that she could work through her feelings and develop an effective career strategy.

For Selene this involved some therapeutic work. She needed to revisit some bad advice that she received as a child from her parents "not to make waves" or "make other people mad." After revisiting how that made her feel as a child, I suggested (perhaps not as gently as I might have) that this was definitely not a good strategy for success in corporate America. When someone steals your work, you have to defend yourself. There are times in life when you have to make waves, and you *will* make people mad. Building a successful career is not a love-in. The goal is not to make everyone love you. It can take courage not to back down in the face of a threat. As Eleanor Roosevelt once astutely commented, "You gain strength, courage, and confidence by every experience in which you really stop to look fear in the face." Roosevelt also believed that you need to "do what you feel in your heart to be right—for you'll be criticized anyway. You'll be damned if you do and damned if you don't."

What Selene needed was permission to fight back. Once she felt comfortable with her right to assert herself, she prepared a memorandum to this woman's manager detailing her indiscretions and why those actions were inappropriate and wrong, scheduled a meeting with the young woman's manager, and elicited his promise to monitor his employee's actions more closely. Comfortable that she had defended her rights and territory, Selene was able to return to her work with greater peace of mind and more confidence in her ability to succeed in the face of threats.

Controlling and Using Your Emotions

The flip side of anger is depression and passivity. From a psychological perspective, depression is a disease of helplessness. It is transacted within the context of powerlessness and pessimists. Although pessimists might be more "realistic," optimists tend to be more successful and have more fun.

This is not to imply that you need to "put on a happy face" or paste smiley faces all over your workspace. Nor do you need to engage in naïve self-affirmations (such as "I'm getting better and better every day, in every way"). However, if you have depressive tendencies, you do need to monitor your self-talk to guard against convincing yourself that any and all effort is basically hopeless. A positive attitude, along with the resilience to rebound from setbacks, is an important predictor of ultimate success or failure. As Henry Ford once commented, "Whether you think you can or think you can't—you are right."

Your feelings can be your ally or your enemy. You must learn to use them to create and accomplish meaningful goals, rather than engage in self-sabotage. Between feeling and productive action lies rational thought. Before acting spontaneously on negative feelings, take some time to calm down and then develop and implement an effective course of action.

Rule 6: Take Calculated Risks

We are often raised with rules, admonitions, and the consequences of disobedience. Look both ways before you cross the street. (You could get hit by a car.) Don't talk to strangers. (You might get kidnapped or worse.) Don't eat unwrapped candy at Halloween. (You might get poisoned.) Wear your hat and boots and gloves in the cold. (So you won't catch pneumonia.) Don't run too fast. (You might fall.)

Good, sound advice from concerned and responsible parents who want their kids to be protected from danger. Good rules to remember and pass along to your own kids. But when those rules and regs translate into a more global message that it's dangerous to take any risks at all, you also end up limiting your rewards.

No Risk, No Reward

When it comes to building a career in the competitive work world, you have to be willing to take risks in order to reap the rewards you seek. You also have to know how to differentiate real danger from fantasy. Not every stranger is dangerous. Nor is every job change or career change a high-wire act. Information is key. You can arm yourself with knowledge.

John was a senior VP with a prestigious accounting firm. After nearly two decades in the business, he was passed over for partnership and told that he didn't have the "personality" or "presence" to be a partner. What they meant was that John was a highly competent professional who could be trusted to do the work he was given. But he was also a very anxious and insecure man who was afraid to assert himself. The partners in his firm were all "rainmakers." They thrived on the challenge of bringing in new business. John was a people pleaser. He tried to make people happy, to adapt to their needs, and to avoid confrontation. Everybody liked him and even respected him. The senior partners in his firm just didn't think he had the "chutzpah" (guts) to succeed at the top. John perceived this as a shortcoming and agreed with them. He wasn't aggressive enough for the role.

What John really wanted to do was get out of corporate America altogether and start a small retail business. He had the skill set to do that. Because he was amiable and friendly, he also had some of the personality traits. What he didn't have was the confidence or the courage to take the financial risk. Despite his ambition, he was never able to achieve any real career satisfaction because he was too afraid to take any real emotional or financial risks. If not for this fatal flaw, he would have been content to buy a retail franchise operation and live out his dream of owning his own business. Ironically, he had the business acumen and skills to know how to evaluate different franchise opportunities and make sound investment decisions. But his enormous fear and self-doubt held him back.

Know Your Risk Tolerance

One key to successful risk-taking is to know your risk tolerance. To do that you must be able to evaluate the potential consequences of your decisions and be able to live with the worst-case scenario. What many otherwise ambitious careerists fail to realize is that *not taking a risk is also a risk*. There is a risk involved in *not trying*. There is risk involved in *not changing*. Along with the risk of failing, there is also the risk of regret.

Archimedes believed that you need only two things to move the world: a lever and a place to stand. Your lever is yourself: the sum total of your personality, talents, interests, and values. Vocationally speaking, your place to stand is wherever you decide to plant your feet in the world of work—whether it be in the courtroom, in the laboratory, in a classroom, on stage, or in front of the computer. It is the place where you feel comfortable enough to practice your craft, exercise your skill, or demonstrate your leadership.

Do You Know the Secrets of Career Success? Thought-Starter Worksheet

1. How do you define success?

   Work that has personal meaning; that you are good at; that allows for growth & pays well.

2. Do you think success (as you define it) will make you happy?

   In part

3. How important is money to your career success?

   Pretty important but i'm not looking to get rich

4. How much money do you need to be happy?

   Enough to feel comfortable and to travel once a year at least

5. How long will it take you to make that much money?

   No idea

6. Does your definition of success include promotions and upward mobility? If so, how hard will you have to work to make that kind of progress?

   I want to work for myself

7. Do you enjoy the work you do? Why or why not?

   Yes but I feel restrained by my boss and understimulated

(continues)

(continued)

8. Would it be easier to put in the kind of hours success required if you liked your work more?

NO

9. Do you consider your work meaningful? Why or why not?

Yes. Helping people without a voice in the community.

10. Is doing meaningful work important to you?

Yes

11. If you considered your work more meaningful, do you think you might be more successful?

NO

12. Would you like to make a career change in order to pursue more interesting or meaningful work?

Yes

13. If so, do you know what area you'd switch to?

Gallery owner

14. What are your obstacles to making a career transition?

Money

Experience

15. Is there any way to transfer some of your current skills and experiences to a new field so that you won't have to take a huge pay cut?

16. Do you consider more schooling an investment in your future? Or a waste of good money?

Investment

17. Is there any degree or training you'd find enjoyable that would also enhance your employability? What is it?

Yes. Or Starting a business. Working in a gallery.

18. Do you participate in any community or volunteer activities that are particularly fulfilling? What are they?

19. Do you have any hobbies you feel passionate about? What are they?

Photography. Sometimes.

20. Do your extracurricular activities provide any clues as to possible vocational choices?

Artmarking

(continues)

(continued)

21. Do you believe that career satisfaction and success are polar opposites—that more satisfying work comes with a vow of poverty? If so, where did you get that idea?

NO

22. Do you know any people who make a lot of money and love their jobs, too?

23. What do they have that you don't?

24. Do you know what kind of work would make you happy? If so, is there a good reason why you aren't pursuing it?

25. If you don't know what kind of work would make you happy, do you know how to figure that out?

26. Have you ever worked with a career counselor to assist you with this decision?

27. How committed are you to your own career happiness?

____

____

28. Do you believe that success and satisfaction can go together?

____

29. If you answered "no" to the preceding question, have you ever tried to integrate the two?

____

CHAPTER 3

Fail(ure) Is Not a Four-Letter Word

Aim high enough and you can always fall on your face.

—Laurence Shames, *The Hunger for More*

When, oh when, will we learn to honor error? To understand that goofs are the only way to step forward, that really big goofs are the only way to leap forward?

—Tom Peters, *The Pursuit of Wow!*

For decades, I kept having the same dream: It was the day of the final exam. I'd never been to class before. I couldn't find the room and was totally unprepared for the test.

Maureen Gold, the director of Baxter Healthcare Corporation's career center in Deerfield, Illinois, admits to having her own version of this almost-universal nightmare about performance and competence. "Final exams are checkpoints where some authority passes judgment on your work," says Gold. "They're a rite of passage. You can't make it to the next step until someone tells you you're OK."

As an adult, you might discover that your work life is putting a new spin on some age-old fears. When Chicago writer Judy Markey informally polled a diverse group of professionals about their current career nightmares, she discovered that many competent people share an anxious underside.

Take, for example, the teacher who dreams she's walked into a classroom of unruly students and doesn't have a single skill to calm down her wild charges. Or the builder who dreams he's grabbed the wrong set of blueprints and built the wrong shelving and cabinets in someone's home. Then there's the accountant whose nightmare revolves around omitting some numbers on a tax form, being discovered by the IRS, and losing most of his clients. And how about the pastor who, in his nighttime angst, walks up to the pulpit in a church packed with worshippers, only to discover that he has nothing to say? No sermon. No words of inspiration. No tidbits of wisdom. Nothing.

This last nightmare is similar to another archetypal fear-of-exposure dream: the one where you're standing naked and exposed before an audience you want desperately to impress. This is probably why a pianist sometimes dreamed she was sitting on stage before a concert stark naked. Or why, on the night before he was expected to deliver an important paper, a doctor dreamed he was at the lectern with no clothes on and his mouth glued shut.

These nighttime dramas reveal, in all their angst-ridden glory, the imperfections that most of us take elaborate precautions to hide. While the rest of the world imagines you're firmly in control of your destiny, your dreams remind you how fallible you really are. Fortunately, these nightmares seldom prove real. Despite the castle of catastrophe you might insist on building in your head, no awful mistake is waiting to rear its ugly head and ambush your career ambitions when you least expect it. Granted, horror stories do happen. But most mistakes are recoverable. However embarrassing, life goes on, and so will you.

Look at Bill Clinton. He was almost driven from the Oval Office in total disgrace because of his sordid sexual affair with a White House intern (whose name will live in infamy). Fast-forward a few years and he is still a popular, much-sought-after public speaker who will undoubtedly have his own television show one day.

Former television newscaster Mary Nissenson Scheer, who worked for NBC News in New York, remembers sharing a particularly embarrassing moment with millions of television viewers. She was pinch-hitting for one of the regular news anchors, who was out sick for the day. It was her first time on national television and her first experience with a teleprompter. While a Freudian interpretation is tempting, nervousness and inexperience are probably what account for Nissenson Scheer's gaffe. At least let's hope that's what caused her to refer to Jimmy Carter's "peanut farm" as a "penis farm," instead.

She can laugh about the incident now, but it wasn't exactly the national television debut she was hoping for. Still, it didn't turn out to be a career-stopper. Surviving the relentless ribbing that trailed her for months was probably the more difficult task. On the bright side, an incident like that can teach you to develop a sense of humor about yourself—pronto!

In our achievement-obsessed society, success and failure are often viewed as opposites. Actually, though, they're part of a continuum. Risk is implied in striving. Every time you make the effort to succeed, you run the risk of failing.

The Thrill of Defeat?

Glen Hiner, the CEO of Owens-Corning Fiberglas Corporation, a $3 billion Toledo-based company, believes in "celebrating" failure rather than maligning it. This isn't an exercise in corporate masochism; it's simply a recognition that the painful lessons learned from failure can pave the way to greater success. That's why Hiner immediately took an $800 million tax write-off on an asbestos litigation case after taking over the helm at Owens-Corning in 1992. He recognized that past failures were holding back his management team from trying new things. He wanted them to put the failure behind them rather than continue to dwell on its consequences.

The head of Nomura Securities, one of Japan's wealthiest companies, shares Hiner's positive outlook on failure. Although it might sound strange, he's concerned that Nomura hasn't had enough failures. Why? He believes that failures force you to develop new ways of thinking and doing things, whereas success, on the other hand, can make you complacent. Instead of looking at and experimenting with new ideas, it encourages you to take the easy way out by endlessly trying to duplicate your past victories.

The professors who run the Harvard MBA program agree with this perspective. That's why their students study failed companies. The experts at this prestigious graduate school know you can learn a lot by understanding where other people went wrong. They say copying someone else's formula for success is unlikely to yield as great a payoff because the competition has already captured the market.

Review the life story of any highly accomplished individual and you'll almost always find a history of failures and recoveries. Usually, the person is someone who was determined to succeed against the odds. Abraham Lincoln is my favorite example of this determination. "Honest Abe's" public report card reads like the record of an "F" student. Born into poverty, he failed in business twice, lost eight elections, and suffered a nervous breakdown before becoming one of this country's greatest presidents.

Why did he persist?

"A duty to strive is the duty of us all," Lincoln said. "I felt a call to that duty."

In chapter 2, I talked about why having a dream, a sense of mission, or a calling is so important for success. Having a greater goal helps you cope with failures, too, by allowing you to place individual setbacks into a larger context. When you believe that your goals are truly worth pursuing, you'll have the desire and momentum to keep going, rather than cave in, in the face of obstacles.

For example, it took my brother Edward Hirsch 10 years to get his first book of poetry in print with a major publisher. Then, its very first week on the shelves, the book was trashed by a reviewer on the front page of the *New York Times Book Review.* This beginning was ominous; but in some ways, it was fortuitous. Having survived a treacherous review early on, Hirsch now is much less afraid of what reviewers will say about his work. Although he still (obviously) prefers praise, he also knows that he can survive the criticism. That "failure" taught him another important lesson: compassion. He's well-known among his writing colleagues for his generosity toward their work. Even when he criticizes them publicly, he never does so in a mean-spirited way.

Common Causes of Career Failure

Failure can be a genuine springboard to success if you allow yourself to learn the lessons it has to teach. You can begin that process by understanding some of the more common reasons failures occur and by learning from the experience of others who have used their defeats to grow and succeed.

Politics

Every successful career is a competitive struggle. Women who hope to break down barriers in traditionally male-dominated fields need a very tough skin and a willingness to engage in power politics. When sportscaster Pam Ward was still struggling for acceptance in "the business," an agent asked her to send him a tape. After the agent watched her tape, he declined to represent her. "He said, 'Look, you are really good, but cosmetically, you're not there.'"

She swore that she would prove him wrong. And eventually she did, recently becoming the first woman to do play-by-play for a college football game. Although it took Ward 10 years to land her first national network job, she persevered through early failures to become an anchor at ESPN.

"I can't tell you how many people told me I would never make it," Ward says. But she was determined to "find the door and kick it in."

Many of her colleagues were initially uncomfortable with her; now many have grown to respect her energy, ambition, and skill. After all, this is a woman who spent her youth imitating Pat Summerall and dreaming of becoming the first woman to announce for the NFL. This is not to say that Pam Ward doesn't have her detractors. Many viewers are still not completely comfortable with a woman sportscaster. Her deep voice and in-your-face style can get on their nerves. And her performances are, undoubtedly, held up to a greater level of scrutiny than the male reporters' are. But, in the final analysis, she will surely turn out to be one of those pioneering women who refused to buy into the notion that football is a man's birthright or that men are born with some innate knowledge of the game that women cannot acquire. She will also disprove the theory that, as a woman, you have to be a former Miss America to be a successful sportscaster. And that—politics notwithstanding—competent women can, indeed, succeed in a man's world. But it takes a very resilient woman such as Pam Ward to bounce back from the kind of rejections and failures she often encountered en route to success.

The Wrong Job

In many cases, poor performance (and sometimes termination) results from a mismatch between an individual and the job he or she is expected to do. Although it's easy to fall into the trap of berating yourself or blaming your employer for the trouble, you need to examine its root causes.

Consider a transportation manager whose career derailed when she joined forces with her company's Midwest operations. In reviewing the circumstances that led to her discharge, the manager realized that the position she held hadn't allowed her to capitalize on her strengths in opening up and developing new markets because the territory she took over was well established.

To correct her course and chart a new direction, she decided to carefully target jobs at companies where she'd be responsible for the development of new territories. Approaching age 50, she knows she can't afford to make another such mistake. By targeting roles that will let her play to her strengths, she hopes to be able to shine more in her next position. It will take some inner fortitude, though, to keep herself from taking another inappropriate position out of financial desperation. If she fails to heed the lesson she's learned too well, she might doom herself to repeat the mistakes of the past. Let's hope not. Facing this same dilemma again at age 55 or 60 is certainly not the future she desires for herself.

"Accidental careerists" (people who fell into rather than chose their professions) are most vulnerable to this kind of career failure. If you fit this profile, you might discover that your career path is more a reflection of who wanted you than what you wanted to do. As a result, you can end up plagued by a halfhearted commitment that makes you lazy and unmotivated. What you really need is a dream and a goal of your own.

A property manager for a complex of apartment buildings lost three jobs in as many years. The problem: her lethargic attitude, which translated into mediocre customer service, poor service contracts (she was too "lazy" to negotiate harder), and an unmotivated support staff (they took their cues from her "leadership" style). To get off that treadmill of mediocrity, she needed to identify and pursue more stimulating and meaningful work. In her sessions with a career counselor, she realized that she needed a more "intellectual" profession. Because teaching and academia appealed most to her, she took the initiative to go to graduate school for a Ph.D. in English literature. She hopes to become a university professor—a career plan that's likely to keep her self-motivated for years to come.

Boss Trouble

A marketing manager who has the bad habit of getting fired every nine months because of personality conflicts with her bosses needs to figure out what's happening before she destroys her entire career. After three premature terminations, she's already having trouble finding new employers who are willing to hire her. They see her job-hopping history as a giant red flag.

Although it's easy to blame your difficulties on all those stupid, incompetent executives, not every boss is a stupid, bumbling fool just because he or she can't get along with you. However painful it might be for you to acknowledge the problem, you aren't doing yourself any favors by exonerating yourself from blame. In fact, when you shift total responsibility for your career problem to "them," you create additional problems for yourself. The truth is, you'll gain more control by owning up to whatever portion of the problem really does belong to you.

Troubling, repetitive patterns in your work history should send up a personal red flag, indicating that you have a problem that needs fixing. If the problem centers around "bosses" or authority issues, you might be staring at some unresolved childhood conflict you have with less-than-perfect parents. Self-employment can help solve the problem. If you're not the entrepreneurial type, however, you'll need another solution. Professional counseling is usually the best answer. But if you can't afford or are afraid of it, you can start tackling the issues on your own by developing insight into your motivations and behaviors.

Writing teacher Gerissa French in Chicago believes you can achieve better self-understanding through a technique she calls "Discovery Write." Here's how this exercise works:

1. Make a list of all the bad bosses you've ever had.
2. Below each name, write down any symbols, objects, or phrases you associate with the person.
3. Put a plus or minus sign next to each symbol, object, or phrase to symbolize whether you think positively or negatively about it.
4. Count up the minus signs. The person with the most blemishes will be your writing subject.
5. Write a character sketch or story about that person. Make it as negative as you want. Write down everything you hate, fear, and

would like to change about that person. Don't hold anything back. (The key here is not to edit your thoughts and feelings.)

6. Put your story away for a day or two. After you've let it settle a while, review what you wrote. How does it look after you've vented your feelings? How true do you think your feelings are to the reality of that person?
7. Now, go to the person on your list with the second most minus signs and complete the same exercise.
8. Compare the first story to the second. Are there any similarities? Think about the two people you're investing with so much negative energy. How similar are they? How different? Are you sure? (If someone you know and trust knows both your subjects, you might want to ask them to review your story. Do their perceptions match up with yours? Or are your fantasies out of control?)
9. Think about the traits that really trigger your hostilities and drive you crazy. Are they similar to those of any of your family members? If so, you've found the link between your bosses and your childhood history, an important first step toward resolving the conflict.

You can also do this exercise in reverse. Start with a family member who has a lot of minuses in your book and write a story or character sketch of that person. After expressing your unedited feelings and perceptions, you should be better able to figure out how your childhood conflicts might be playing out in your work life with bosses.

French experienced a personal epiphany regarding a family member who'd been inculcated with the message that he was an "ugly duckling." To compensate for that diminished status, her relative often "strutted his stuff"—behaving more like a bantam rooster than an ugly duckling. To this day, French has a love-hate relationship with rooster-type men.

What does all this have to do with your career? By knowing what kind of people and behaviors trigger your emotional vulnerabilities, you can steer clear of those types altogether. Or you can take measures to ensure that your working relationships with such individuals develop along the lines of healthy professionalism, not as reruns of some well-worn emotional tapes from your childhood.

Wrong Employer

Some people are simply better suited to self-employment than to working for a company. Figuring out that there's an entrepreneur lurking in your soul can be the solution to a long string of unhappy jobs.

Hollywood movie producer David Brown, whose credits include such blockbusters as *Jaws* and *Cocoon,* considers himself an expert on the subject of failure. Brown was fired from four jobs (including two top posts at 20th Century Fox) before figuring out that he's too much of a risk-taker for conventional corporate life. Once he came to that realization, he formed his own production company, where he's free to be as creative and daring as he chooses. But it took four failed tries as a "wage slave" to figure out that he couldn't find the solution to his employment problems in corporate America.

Of course, he'll never repeat that same employment mistake if he can help it. As former baseball catcher and sportscaster Joe Garagiola says: "Experience is mistakes you won't make anymore."

Too Much Self-Confidence

Harry Truman once said, "The only things worth learning are the things you learn after you know it all."

Success can be a powerful aphrodisiac, especially when accompanied by money, fame, and power. It can lure you into thinking you're omnipotent: that nothing and no one can touch you.

Witness the case of boxer Mike Tyson, who didn't have the character or inner strength to handle his own success. Behold also the downfalls of Jim Bakker, Leona Helmsley, Michael Milken, and Ivan Boesky, all of whom have had the opportunity to contemplate the error of their ways from inside a jail cell. Prison time must have its pluses: Boesky found God and professes to want to be a rabbi; Tyson converted to Islam; Milken discovered the joys of public service and has been seen escorting poor kids to baseball games; Bakker has repented for his sins and wants his pulpit back to try again. Ms. Helmsley, on the other hand, seemed sorry most of all that she got caught.

The Watergate folks also seemed to find religion in the wake of their downfall. Whether these religious conversions are real remains to be seen.

Inexperience

Because entrepreneurs take so many risks through uncharted territory, it's not surprising that they experience a fair share of failures. When *Inc.* magazine compiled its latest list of the 500 fastest-growing private companies in America, they discovered that the founders of these businesses usually needed a few tries to get it right. Many had started out in different enterprises; and of those initial start-ups, one-third died untimely deaths. One-half were sold. The founders didn't hit on the right formulas immediately, but they lived (nonetheless) to sell another day.

What often differentiates entrepreneurs from the rest of us is not only their fearlessness toward risk and failure. It is also their relentless ability to see opportunity everywhere.

When Nicholas Hall read an article that chronicled the ups and downs of his fellow entrepreneurs, he took particular note of the high percentage of startup failures. Hall was no stranger to startup failure, but he always enjoyed the journey in both the good times and the bad. That's when he got the idea to start a Web site called "Startupfailures—The Place for Bouncing Back." This online community supports entrepreneurs through the experience of a startup failure. Its purpose is to take the stigma out of failure, help entrepreneurs rebound from their setback, and "get back into the game and the action." As Hall says, "The only true failure is never trying."

Mastering an activity can be its own reward, despite the outcome. I have a feeling this is a lesson that Ellen Ripstein already knows.

Ripstein used to be called "the Susan Lucci of Crossword Puzzles." Before capturing the American Crossword Puzzle Tournament Title in 2001, Ripstein had finished among the top five for 18 years in a row without ever emerging victorious. (Soap opera buffs may recall that Lucci was nominated for an Emmy award 19 times before she finally won the coveted trophy in 1999 for her work as an actress on "All My Children.") The concentration, skill, and discipline it takes to win this tournament are nearly unimaginable. For Ripstein, who researches and proofreads puzzles and word games for a living, the tournament is an intensely competitive event and no joking matter. Just to give you a little perspective, she is capable of completing the Saturday *New York Times* puzzle in less than five minutes and the Sunday version in 10 to 15 minutes.

Bad Timing

Some of failure's best lessons are in the realm of self-knowledge. All that soul-searching anchors information in ways that are both memorable and character-building.

Olympic speed skater Dan Jansen's sister Jane died of leukemia on the day of his 500-meter race in Calgary in 1988. Had the fates been kind, Jansen would have won that 500-meter race he dedicated to his sister, or at least the 1,000-meter race he skated four days later. Instead, he stumbled twice and went down in defeat. You can write his mistakes off to grief and be partly right. But it wasn't just sadness that made him stumble. It was fear of success, too, and possibly survivor's guilt. He just didn't feel right celebrating a victory so soon after his sister's death. It was more important to mourn her passing.

Six years later, he felt more ready and deserving of the honor. In fact, he felt worthy enough to set a new Olympic world record in the 1,000-meter race at Lillehammer and to take victory laps with his daughter Jane nestled in his arms. Although such well-deserved victories are obviously heartwarming, Jansen believes that the battle to accomplish your goals is more important than any medal or award. Some of his fans agree. One of his favorite post-Olympian memories came from a well-wisher who told him, "You would've been a hero whether you won the race or not." Like Jansen, she believed that his ability to persist in the face of adversity was every bit as admirable as the medal. Jansen's father agrees, saying that the way his son handles his defeats is every bit as impressive as the way he handles victory. This is not about being a good loser. It is about the dignity of wholehearted commitment and effort.

Prejudice

Some failures are the result of ignorance—not your own, but other people's. Such ignorance typically reveals itself in the form of racism, sexism, or ageism.

A successful accountant in Philadelphia was his employer's "favorite son" right up until the day the company discovered he was gay and summarily discharged him. What resulted was a down-and-dirty lawsuit that the accountant eventually lost. But in the process, he gained something more important: a sense of integrity. Never again would he hide his sexual orientation. He vowed that from then on, he'd always live an openly homosexual life. He also decided to establish his own practice. He was gratified to discover that most clients care little about their accountant's sexual orientation and a great deal about his or her ability to save them tax dollars. This knowledge made him much more secure about his professional future and place in the human community.

For people who have felt the need to hide their religion, sexual preferences, age, or other sensitive information from their employers, to have that information come out into the open can be liberating, even if they end up losing a job as a result (which, hopefully, they won't).

Although how much personal information you reveal should always be your choice, you won't always have that luxury. Should you find yourself on the wrong end of prejudice and ignorance, you can use it to affirm your essential values. Standing up for who you are and what you believe can armor you with self-knowledge and resiliency that will make it difficult for anyone to successfully undermine you.

So the next time someone doesn't like who you are or what you stand for, remember that it's really their problem, not yours. They're entitled to what they believe, but their beliefs can't diminish you unless somewhere deep down you think they're right.

Poor Support Systems

The power of community was probably the single greatest variable in the success and failure of Oskar Schindler, a German industrialist during World War II, whose exploits have been recorded for posterity by writer Thomas Kenneally and dramatized by Steven Spielberg in *Schindler's List.*

Schindler was a conniving, manipulative womanizer whose initial goal was to exploit a wartime economy by using the Jewish people as cheap labor to staff his start-up enamelware company. His motivation was strictly economic self-interest. What he didn't bargain for was the incredible father-son relationship he would develop with his chief accountant Itzhak Stern, and how Schindler's desire to please his surrogate father would so transform his psyche.

Stern was an astute businessman who taught Schindler how to make money. In the process, he also taught him love and compassion for the people who brought him profits. Eventually, Schindler's mission to save the people who worked for him became larger and more important than his desire to make money and did, indeed, interfere with his capitalistic motives. By the time the war was over, the wealthy Schindler was a poor man who had managed to save hundreds of lives.

After the war, without his trusted business advisor, Schindler was never able to grow a viable business again. He died a poor man, dependent on the people he'd saved for his own survival. Was Schindler a success or a failure? In his lifetime, Schindler succeeded and failed several times. Financially, he did not succeed. In other ways, it's more difficult to judge. In Israel, he always received a hero's welcome from the people he had saved. In his native country, he was often jeered as a Jew-lover.

Maybe it isn't fair to judge a man's life in terms of some great final curtain call. Schindler's greatest accomplishments occurred in the middle of his life, when a trusted advisor and a nobler purpose created a unique window of opportunity for him to succeed financially. Ironically, at a time when he was most able to achieve financial success, he cared more for something (or someone) else. That Oskar Schindler, a conniving, manipulative womanizer, was capable of such noble acts should give us all pause for thought.

Strong people connections were also at the heart of Dan Jansen's ability to recover from his setbacks at Calgary. Jansen (who credits much of his success to his extensive network of supportive family and friends) uses a technique called the "mental war room," which he learned from sports psychologist Jim Loer. The room is a place he peoples with his favorite memories, photographs, conversations, and even songs. When the outside world threatens to overwhelm his capacity to concentrate, he goes into his "mental war room" for comfort and calm.

If you don't have good support systems available to you during stressful times, failures become an experience of isolation rather than connection. To overcome that sense of alienation, you must force yourself to reach out to others who can help. This can be a risk. People aren't always predictable. Sometimes, trusted buddies turn out to be fair-weather friends while more distant acquaintances move in to fill the breach. As an account-executive client of mine remarked, "You really find out who your friends are when the chips are down."

For this executive, the chips were down on the day her boss at the marketing research company where she worked expressed displeasure with her leadership abilities and gave her 60 days to straighten out. The problem, it turns out, reflected a conflict of values more than a lack of leadership. The account executive has a strong people orientation and tends to lead with her heart as much as her head. Her boss, a vice president, manages strictly in accordance with the numbers on the bottom line. Employee welfare and job security aren't considerations for him. Thus, to avoid being called "too soft," the account executive had to deal with her staff in a manner markedly against her nature.

Soon, she began to question whether she really had the skills to survive in business. Certainly, no one in her company seemed to respect her abilities or regard her future. Her crisis of confidence was so strong that she sought professional assistance to determine whether she needed a career change. As we talked, it became clear that she did need to toughen up emotionally and not take criticism of her abilities quite so seriously. She also needed to realize, though, that the respect she shows to subordinates is a strength, not a weakness. Although it's important to acknowledge and deal with bottom-line concerns, this doesn't have to mean treating others disrespectfully and unfairly.

Strengthened by our conversation, the account executive approached her boss with ideas for improving the bottom line without firing staff. When her boss didn't buy in, she decided to look for a more supportive business environment where her values and style would be more compatible with those of her co-workers.

Turning Failures Around

Most failures are symptoms that you need to make some kind of change. Although it's tempting to see yourself as the victim of bad luck, you'll be better off if you figure out whether you're contributing to your own misfortunes.

Have you ever noticed, for example, that while you always end up on the short end of fate, there are others who always seem to end up on the right side of it? Probably, it's no accident. Find me a person who always seems to be in the "right place at the right time," and I'll show you someone who knows how to recognize and convert opportunities to his or her own advantage.

Blaming your bad luck on someone else is worse yet. It moves the locus of control "out there" where you can't do anything to make it better. What you really need to do is buckle down and figure out how to gain more control.

When you catch yourself falling into the blaming trap, a neon STOP sign should go on in your head. Instead of falling into "poor-me, rotten-you" thinking, ask yourself how you can turn your defeat into a more positive experience. Perhaps you've been unfairly treated. Can you think of ways you could have handled the situation differently? Honestly, were you the stellar, outstanding citizen and employee you're now claiming to be? Did a competitor beat you, perhaps, because he actually had better skills or better connections?

Sometimes we lose out on things we really want because someone knew someone who knew someone who helped your rival gain the inside advantage. You can call it "rotten luck," or you can identify it as a need for better networking or more marketable job skills.

It helps if you can find some humor in your situation. Although he had every right to cry "poor me" a hundred times over, actor George Lopez chose to transform his traumatic childhood experiences into a television laugh track. In the process, he learned the power of self-discovery, resilience, and forgiveness. Although he is the creator and main character in a successful sitcom, his successful ratings are based on the painful reality of a failed childhood from which he is still recovering.

Regardless of the shape and form they take, failures can—and often do—feel like the end of the world. Most failures, however, are temporary setbacks rather than career enders. The key is to be able to overcome the blow to your ego, which almost always occurs, so that you can learn the lessons failure can teach. Invariably, one of these lessons involves humility. No matter how high you climb, you'll always make mistakes. Owning up to those mistakes is part of the process of career growth.

Dr. Spock's Change of Heart

The name "Dr. Spock" was a household word to most baby boomers' parents, who religiously followed his recommendations when rearing their children. Because of his widespread success, Benjamin Spock never anticipated the criticism he'd receive a generation later at the hands of feminists who vehemently disagreed with his advice. After these attacks, Dr. Spock retreated into emotional isolation to determine what had happened. At first he simply nursed his wounds. Once he got past the hurt, though, he began to see his critics' point. He adapted his viewpoint publicly and acknowledged that fathers were equally capable of good child-rearing practices. It was a sign of Dr. Spock's wisdom and strength that he was eventually able to hear the criticism and respond to it appropriately. Otherwise, he would have quickly become an anachronism, a man who could not respond to the call of new times.

Criticisms can be painful but important learning experiences. Sometimes, as in Spock's case, they're well justified. Other times, they're mostly professional jealousy, someone else's sour grapes. In either case, you must learn to find the kernel of truth in what others say about you. More important, you must learn to listen to the voice within yourself. Know what those nagging self-doubts you carry in your head really mean lest you turn them into self-fulfilling prophecy.

Setbacks can show you what not to do again and teach you how to cope with—and grow—from failure. Although you might never embrace failure wholeheartedly, you might find some truth in the cliché that "what doesn't kill you makes you stronger." Having survived your losses, you might discover a newfound power within yourself.

According to Mary Lynn Pulley, the author of *Losing Your Job—Reclaiming Your Soul,* "Probably the most important thing that people can do to avoid feeling like a victim is to not dwell on why something happened...but instead move forward with a sense of hope and imagination toward their future."

It's a Wonderful Life

We all know the movie "It's a Wonderful Life." It is a Christmas classic that is etched into our collective psyche. This film is a story about a man named George Bailey. Although he's a good, honest man always struggling to do the right thing, Bailey questions his life and the choices he's made. Teetering on the brink of despair, he finally concludes that his life has been a failure. Surmising that it might have been better if he had never been born, he contemplates suicide. Thanks to the efforts of a novice angel (determined to get his wings), Bailey discovers that he was not a failure at all—that he did fit into the scheme of life and contributed much to the happiness of other people.

The story behind the story is equally compelling. The original screenplay for this movie grew out of a short story written by Philip Van Doren that, ironically, no one wanted and never got published in that form. Instead, Van Doren published his story as a Christmas card. But director Frank Capra recognized its potential and, in 1946, produced the movie that would become his magnum opus.

Although the movie wasn't initially a commercial disaster, neither was it a commercial success. Despite opening to generally positive reviews, it lost money on its initial release. Time turned out to be its greatest ally. Capra believes that it's because "there's a little George Bailey in all of us." Perhaps it's a message we need to hear again and again. That's why, at least once every year, we thank Jimmy Stewart (and Frank Capra) for reminding us that even if we haven't achieved all of our career and financial goals, there are myriad ways to measure success and still feel good about our lives.

Fail(ure) Is Not a Four-Letter Word Thought-Starter Worksheet

1. What is your experience with failure so far?

   medium

2. Are you afraid to fail?

   Yes

3. Does a fear of failure ever prevent you from trying new things?

   Yes

4. If you weren't afraid of failing, what would you do (or try to do)?

   artist

5. When you were growing up, how did your parents handle your mistakes?

   Shame

6. As a youngster, were you overly critical of your own mistakes? If yes, do you know why?

   Yes. meant I was a loser

7. Do you have a low opinion of your own abilities?

   Yes and no

8. Do you suffer from low self-esteem?

Yes

9. Describe your biggest career failure.

1 Teaching troubled teenagers

2 Selling clothing in a boutique (fired twice)

10. How did it make you feel to fail?

like a loser

11. Do you know why the failure occurred?

1 lack of experience & low self-esteem

2 shy and undermotivated

12. Is there anything you could have done to prevent yourself from failing?

Tried harder

Not giving up

13. Do you consider yourself a perfectionist?

No

14. Do you know the difference between a small mistake and a big one?

Sort of

(continues)

(continued)

15. Do you have a tendency to take yourself too seriously?

Yes

16. Can you think of a time in your life when you learned something important from failure that prevented you from making a similar mistake again?

17. Of all the examples cited in this chapter, whom did you identify with the most? Why?

News caster. Screwed up and was embarrassed but preserevered

18. Of all the examples cited in this chapter, whom did you admire the most? Is there anything you can do to be more like that person?

Dr. Spock

Learn from criticism

19. If you're overly fearful of failure, have difficulty accepting your own mistakes, and/or have trouble recovering from career setbacks, have you considered working with a professional therapist to strengthen your resiliency? Why or why not?

Yes.

CHAPTER 4

Oh No, 50!: Midlife Career Transitions

Why put off until tomorrow what you can put off until the day after tomorrow?

—Mark Twain

We cannot live the afternoon of life according to the program of life's morning.

—Carl Jung

After losing two friends on September 11th, New York Knicks coach Jeff Van Gundy decided that it was time for him to say "Adios" to the sport he loved. Van Gundy wasn't the only one to speed up his retirement. AOL Time-Warner executive Gerald Levin was also so affected by the attacks that he escalated the timetable for his retirement.

But it wasn't just high-profile executives and millionaires who saw "9-11" as an opportunity to re-evaluate their goals and priorities. For Dan, a 54-year-old communications technician, the moment of truth came during the funeral of a family friend. Although he was planning to retire in two years, time suddenly seemed more precious to him than building his retirement nest egg, so he accepted a voluntary buyout. Randy had a similar epiphany. Although he had always planned to retire at 55, watching the twin towers fall forced him to rethink his timetable.

"I always wanted to travel and see the world," Randy said. "All of a sudden it felt like 'now or never.'"

Two days later, Randy quit his job as an accountant and bought a ticket to Australia, where he's learned to appreciate the more leisurely lifestyle. Although he knows he has yet to decide what he wants to do when he gets back from his sabbatical, he is enjoying the time off to regain his composure and perspective.

Although the events of "9-11" might have spawned a number of midlife transitions, they are certainly not new. Such transitions have been around for a while now. When she was 33 years old, Anna Navarro was the director of corporate social responsibility at St. Louis–based Monsanto Company. As the top-ranking female executive in the company, she had a high-profile, high-paying job that would have made many ambitious people drool. But in some fundamental way, it wasn't fulfilling. "I was at the top," says Navarro, "but I was spending my time writing reports and crunching numbers, which I hate, and doing the bureaucratic maneuvering that's essential for a rising executive. I wasn't having very much fun. What I really wanted was to wear casual clothes and make a real difference in the quality of people's lives."

One day during lunch, a male colleague who was about 45 years old started complaining to Navarro about how much he hated his job. He calculated that he had 10 more years to go before he could take early retirement. That conversation really bothered Navarro. Driving home that night, she told herself that if there was a different way to live, she didn't want to wait until she was 55 to discover it. Realizing that, she did something quite miraculous. Without knowing what she wanted to do next, she resigned so that she could figure it out. It wasn't a flip decision. She agonized long and hard before making the move. Her friends thought she was crazy. Her husband tried to talk her out of it. So did the people she worked with, as well as the CEO who had recruited and mentored her.

"You can do anything you want here," he told her. But there was nothing there she wanted to do. Not that she had some perfect vision of what she really wanted. She just needed the time and space to figure it out. A few years of introspection, brainstorming, and research brought her to an awareness that resulted in the founding of Work Transitions, a service based in St. Louis that helps others navigate out of career ruts like the one she was experiencing.

Navarro apparently hit her midlife career crisis early. For most people, it strikes around age 50. Although there's nothing magical about that age, the five-decade mark seems to send out warning signals that it's time to cross some new developmental threshold. At 50, you can no longer pretend that you're young; but if you're healthy, you probably aren't feeling old, either.

This is what it means to be middle-aged. Your youth is definitely behind you, but your most productive years might still be ahead. If you're like most of the 50-year-olds I know, you're probably asking yourself: "How do I really want to spend my time?" The answer to that question is a highly individual one. But the prevalence of midlife career changes makes it unlikely that you'll be alone if you decide that you want to spend the next stage of your life doing something different than you did before.

Are You Just Waiting for a Pension?

To make the right decisions during this phase of life, you need to understand the new philosophical view of work that Navarro teaches. The days when a person could join an organization and receive automatic job security, benefits, pay raises, and promotions are gone forever, she says. Work is structured differently now. The key today is to know how to survive and grow in the midst of change. To do that, you must take responsibility for managing your own career.

This can be a hard message to learn late in the work game, especially if you've been entrusting your career to your employer all these years. You might discover (if you haven't already done so) that the job market isn't cooperating with your desires anymore. Outplacement counselors know this mentality all too well. In every workshop we teach, there is inevitably someone whose only career ambition was to get a full pension and retire.

If you've spent your career stockpiling money and years of service rather than marketable skills, losing your job can be a downright catastrophe. It's daunting to face a discriminatory job market when you're in the twilight of your career and lack both self-confidence and a set of abilities that employers value. It makes for a lot of bitterness, insecurity, and cynicism.

There are lucky professionals who manage to make it safely to retirement without any hitches. But even these folks have been learning some rude life lessons. Many are finding retirement to be unaffordable financially or emotionally—or both. As one 55-year-old former sales manager commented after only three months of retirement, "It's OK for a summer vacation. But I can't spend the rest of my life chasing a ball around the golf course. I have to do something more productive."

Ditto for a 60-year-old data-processing specialist who returned to work part time after less than a year out. "I could only pot so many plants," she says. "Once the garden was finished, I needed a little more mental stimulation."

The idea that every person's life should begin with education and end with leisure (with an extended period of work in the middle) is too narrowly proscribed to meet the complexity of modern adult lives and desires. For starters, it ignores the possibility that some people might actually enjoy their work and want to go on doing it for as long as they're physically and mentally able. And that even those who don't like their jobs might prefer tackling a new challenge over spending the rest of their years rocking on the front porch.

A New Phase of Life

New York gerontologist Lydia Bronte, who wrote, *The Longevity Factor: The New Reality of Long Careers and How It Can Lead to Richer Lives* (1993, HarperCollins), posits the existence of a whole new stage in life between ages 50 and 75. She calls this period "second middle age" and says that adults in this phase need fulfilling activities to motivate them, especially because people are living longer and are healthier today.

"When adults over 50 realize just how much time there is left to accomplish new things, a whole new sense of adventure takes over," says Judy Rosemarin, a career counselor with Sense-Able Strategies in Roslyn, New York. "It can be a very exciting time."

Anita Lands, a New York City career counselor who specializes in working with older adults, sees the age-50 transition as a time of greater introspection. "A lot of people start questioning what's really important to them," says Lands, "and they make some tradeoffs—usually in terms of money and upward mobility for greater satisfaction."

Rosemarin agrees. "People over 50 are usually looking for better ways to integrate who they are with how they make a living," she says. "They want to use and develop some parts of themselves that they may have neglected in earlier years."

In this era of rampant layoffs and forced retirements, these re-evaluations are sometimes forced on people. After 25 years in information technology, Cindy lost her job when her employer laid off thousands of workers following the terrorist attacks. For the next six months, the 60-year-old IT professional did everything in her power to find another job. But, in the face of a resounding silence from the job market, she began to daydream about starting her own gourmet food shop.

As months passed with no job offers on the horizon, she began to think more seriously about launching a new career and discovered that the more she thought about it, the more excited and energized she became. So she put together a business plan, raised some seed money, and lined up some bankers. As her new career unfolded, she began to see the silver lining in her situation. The way she sees it these days, she was given the freedom to find out what else she wanted to do. And she admits she's having a lot of fun doing it.

How Old Are You?

Often, a crisis such as a layoff or forced retirement leads people to shift from "cultural adulthood" to "emotional adulthood," says Steven Baum, a gerontologist and psychologist in private practice in Detroit. Baum, the author of *Growing Up at Any Age* (1994, Health Communications), believes that people are culturally railroaded into accepting artificial limits that have nothing to do with their individual abilities and shortcomings. True adulthood arrives, he says, when you're able to develop a personal definition of what is meaningful rather than submit to socially and economically prescribed set points.

Retirement at age 65 is one of these arbitrary set points. Although many arbitrarily assume that people are "old" at 65, there is no biological imperative that makes it true. Some people are emotionally (and even physically) old at age 35, whereas others are young at 75. Consider the late actress Jessica Tandy and her husband, actor Hume Cronyn. In the film *Cocoon,* they teamed up to play an aging couple given the gift of renewed youth. To prepare for their roles, the then-75ish pair had to be taught how to "act old" because they had too much spring in their walks and gleam in their eyes. In a wonderful ironic twist, this energetic couple had to learn how to look worn out and worn down in order to fit the traditional stereotype of the elderly as doddering and frail.

When you turn 65, you don't suddenly become a gray-haired monster. The reason 65 is the traditional retirement age has more to do with an economic formula based on company pension plans and Social Security regulations than the norms of human aging. What that means, however, is that you might get kicked out of the workforce before you're actually ready to go.

Worth magazine believes that the whole concept of retirement should be retired. Why? First of all, it isn't financially feasible for most people. The math just doesn't work. Nor does it make most people happy. To have years of idleness and leisure isn't everyone's idea of the ultimate good time. Some people prefer to remain active, contributing participants to society. "Retirement isn't about doing what you want and it certainly isn't a Golden Age," according to the magazine. "Retirement is a weird social experiment...its collapse will be a triumph for common sense.

Indeed, on the day after your 65th birthday, you might feel much the way you did the day before, except that you don't have a job anymore. Rather than slip into the role of the old person that society has declared you to be, take stock of how you personally feel and how you want the next phase of your work life to look.

"Most of us tend to think of retirement as the end of the story," says Lydia Bronte. "But people who retire wake up the next morning, much as they've always done, and start another day of life. Retirement is another phase in life, not the end of it."

For increasing numbers of professionals, retirement isn't the end of life; it isn't even the end of work. Instead, it's the end of a specific job or career with a specific company. As one 50-year-old former IBMer says, "The key to retirement is to do it early and often."

Be Imaginative

In the movie *Six Degrees of Separation,* an ambitious young man pretends to be "Paul Poitier," son of famed actor Sidney Poitier. As Paul, he worms his way into the good graces of a wealthy New York art dealer and his wife who, despite their glamorous lives, long for greater excitement. Passionately weaving a tale of words, he touches the wife profoundly, making her think more clearly and deeply than ever before about the emptiness of the life she's leading. Without realizing that he's speaking their truth as well as his own, "Paul Poitier" teaches them, "Imagination makes the art of self-examination bearable."

Although I can't recommend this character's method of fabricating a whole past life, he demonstrates how the power of a vision can captivate and enliven both the present and the future. When looking at your own lifeline, imagining a different existence than the one you've lived so far can move you to a whole new place. Rather than impose self-limiting beliefs on yourself, why not learn to recognize and live more comfortably with your choices and desires?

William Gold did just that, even though it meant going against the grain of what others thought he should do with his later years. Gold owned a heating and plumbing installations business in Quincy, Illinois, for 40 years. A master craftsman, he always enjoyed hands-on work more than business management. In the early 1980s, changes in the economic climate made it difficult for a meticulous craftsman to do work in the way he so enjoyed. So, at age 65, he elected to close his business altogether. But he couldn't afford to retire and, in truth, he didn't want to. His work was one of the great passions of his life.

Searching for new options, he considered the obvious choice: consulting. Certainly, he knew enough about government rules and regulations to consult to others. But the field didn't really appeal to him. He was more of a hands-on type. To everyone's amazement (and amid a hail of protests from well-meaning friends and family), he went to work with the crew of men he'd once hired. And to everyone else's surprise, he loved every minute of his new job. Being the oldest member of the crew didn't exempt him from having to do physical labor (although the younger men did help him with some of the lifting and carrying). But on the road, he was "one of the boys" again and as involved and productive as he'd ever been. More than anything else, he loved feeling useful. That, for him, was the true bottom line.

His work was so important to him that he would have done it whether or not he got paid. He could never walk into a room without remodeling it in his mind's eye. At his synagogue, he took the single-handed initiative to remodel the rabbi's study, even though he didn't get paid for the work. And when he visited a cemetery and saw that the cast-iron gates were broken, he rented a welding torch and used his own money to fix them. When asked why, he responded simply: "It needed to be done."

Gold died at age 75. He worked up until three weeks before his death. On his last official day on the job, he was part of a crew that was remodeling the hospital emergency room. When he was done, he turned in his tools, walked around the corner, and checked himself into the hospital, where he was operated on for cancer. His working days might have been over, but in his mind, he was still on the job. Even on his deathbed, he and his brother Ben were joyously scribbling and planning installations.

Gerontologists Paul Costa and Robert McCrae of the National Institute of Aging in Washington, D.C., pinpoint "openness to experience" as the single most important lifelong trait for successful aging. So don't buy into the idea that everything goes downhill once you reach a certain age. Instead, why not try to recapture some of the spirit of adventure you had before all those financial responsibilities started weighing down your choices?

The Health Factor

Good health is obviously a wild card that determines how active and productive you can be in your latter years. But, for many people, the expectation of physical deterioration is more myth than reality. Not everyone ages in exactly the same way or according to identical timetables. Attitude (and, in some cases, inactivity) might play a larger role than most people yet realize.

In 1965, at 59 years old, Satchel Paige was obviously too old to play professional baseball. So how did the former Kansas City A's pitcher manage to turn in three scoreless innings in a single game for his team that year? Either he didn't know he was too old, or he was too old to care what other people thought. "How old would you be if you never knew how old you was?" quipped Paige.

Physical age doesn't have to be synonymous with feeling old. Why accept limitations you don't really have to? My friend Mel Marks, a retired marketing consultant who is nearing 70, still runs every day and competes in marathons. Norman Vaughn, an 86-year-old Alaskan adventurer, competes annually in a 1,100-mile dogsled race that has defeated much younger men and women.

What about Dietrich Lamprecht, a 67-year-old former steelworker, who's enjoyed more competitive success in retirement than he ever did in traditional work roles? Lamprecht took up bicycle racing after his employer, Kaiser Steel Co. in Fontana, California, went bankrupt 10 years ago. Spurred on by the joy of competing, Lamprecht won the Masters World Cup in Austria against a field of 2,300 riders from 37 countries. He's also the current U.S. national cyclist champion in his age class. Defying the "one-foot-in-the-grave" stereotype of older adults, he is the picture of health and vitality.

In part, it is the dream of winning and the love of competition that keep him motivated. Like many people, Lamprecht found his calling after retirement, when some of the monetary constraints attached to making a living were removed. Canadian scholar John A.B. McLeish refers to people like him as "Ulyssean adults" because, like Ulysses, they set out on new voyages in their later years.

While some older adults push for new physical adventures, a yearning and quest for creativity might also govern the journey. Marks, for example, has taken up writing and published his first historical work, called *Jews Among the Indians;* corporate attorney Frank Mackey traded in his share of his Little Rock, Arkansas, law practice to begin a new career as an actor. Defying the conventional notions about older adults, these active folks aren't getting ready to die. They're just learning how to live.

Judy Rosemarin believes that older adults need to recapture some of the curiosity and wonder that children typically bring to their projects. She cites a wonderful inspirational story about her friend Harry Lieberman, who retired from his job as a candy maker after 50 years in the business. One day, the 80-year-old Lieberman was hanging out at the senior center, waiting for his chess partner, who didn't show. To keep busy, Lieberman allowed himself to be persuaded to start painting.

The furthest thing from this man's mind was starting a new career at the age of 80. But he proved to have such a talent for primitive painting that, like Grandma Moses, his work caught the attention of others and started selling. As a result, his next 24 years of life (!) proved enormously productive. When he was 100 years old, a New York publishing house signed him to a seven-year contract to illustrate one of their calendars. Lieberman died with three years left to go on the contract. Lieberman didn't set out to emulate the life of Grandma Moses, the American primitive artist from upstate New York. She began painting at the age of 75 because she was "too old to work on the farm and too young to sit on the porch." Nevertheless, the similarity of his late-life career path took him down that road anyway.

Later Years Can Be Productive Years

The idea of starting a whole new career at 60, 70, or even 80 might seem strange at first. But if you recognize that development doesn't stop just because your birthday has arrived (yet again), you might be pleasantly surprised by how productive and fulfilling your later years turn out to be. The key is to involve yourself in activities you find stimulating, regardless of the financial payoff.

When she was 54 years old, after a long career as a traditional wife and mother, Shirley Brussell went back to school to complete a master's degree in community organization. While studying at the university, she became involved in creating employment programs for older people. At age 56, she served on a volunteer task force to create an employment counseling service for seniors. Twenty-five years later, Brussell heads up Operation Able, a nonprofit organization in Chicago with a $4 million annual budget and 350 employees on its payroll.

For her, retirement is a concept that holds no allure. Instead, she concentrates on planning her future involvements—always thinking in terms of what she wants to learn or where she wants to help. "As long as you feel yourself growing," says Brussell, "you don't feel old."

The desire to keep growing and to give something back to the community fuels many late-life career decisions. For people with that urge, writing and teaching have proved particularly popular options. For inspiration, look at 77-year-old, Pulitzer Prize-winning historian Arthur Schlesinger, Jr., who says, "Writing history is more fun than doing anything else, so I just keep on doing it." For him, intellectual curiosity is a great preservative. Without mental stimulation and activity, he'd be a very unhappy man.

"The beauty of teaching as a second career choice is that it lets you use all the wisdom and experience you've gained through the years," says Judy Rosemarin. "It's fun for people to be able to give some of what they've learned through the years back to others."

For one 51-year-old engineer who's in the midst of a segue from Illinois Bell into teaching computer science, early retirement has felt more like graduation day. "It's as if huge weights have been lifted from my feet and I'm finally free to achieve my potential," she says. While she intends to upgrade her education with a new master's degree, many professionals already have the credentials and knowledge to teach. At 75, a former nuclear physicist discovered he was more than qualified to teach calculus and physics to undergraduate students. As an adjunct professor, he immensely enjoys the classes he teaches. Plus, unlike career academics who are constrained by the need to publish, he's free to focus his time and attention strictly on serving and helping students. It's a wonderful way for him to stay connected to a younger generation without denying his own maturity and experience.

Managing Late Career Change

Job security might be a thing of the past, but there's no reason that job changes and transitions need to be viewed as career failures or the end of the line. If you want or need to continue working, you can take the initiative to develop innovative career strategies that enable you to remain a productive, contributing member of the workforce in your later years.

After a Job Loss

If you're over age 50 and you just lost your job, there's no need to assume that retirement has to be your next step. Rick Ehlers, director of client services for Jarosz and Associates, an outplacement firm in Deerfield, Illinois, encourages older professionals to view job losses as opportunities to do more interesting and meaningful work.

"The current economic climate provides a unique opportunity for older professionals to identify niches for their expertise, rather than worrying about where there are actual job openings," says Ehlers. By way of example, he cites the case of an older candidate who'd been an on-air personality with several major radio networks. At first, the man had trouble finding a job on air in the competitive, youth-oriented world of network radio. So he decided to switch gears to consulting and was able to convince a small Chicago station to create a spot for him. As a consultant, he was able to help station executives with programming decisions, coach on-air personalities, and even work with the sales force to develop strategies. Instead of leaving the industry he loved, he was able to parlay his extensive media expertise into whole new areas of skill and experience. The key was adopting a more independent mind-set.

The reality of age discrimination means that older workers often need to develop more autonomous ways of working rather than rely on a single employer for their whole paycheck. Happily, many experienced professionals seek greater freedom and independence, anyway. If that's your situation, starting your own new venture might be the best way to go, especially if you have lots of ambition and energy left for work.

Col. Harlan Sanders, founder of Kentucky Fried Chicken, was 64 years old when he decided to franchise his restaurant and method of making fried chicken. Ten years later, he had more than 600 franchises operating under the KFC name. Not surprisingly, Col. Sanders believed that mandatory retirement was a waste of valuable brain power, talent, and energy. He thought it should be eliminated.

Speaking before the U.S. Congressional Committee on Aging in 1977, he made the following comments:

> *I'm not against retirement for people who want it. But retirement's just not for me. I believe a man will rust out quicker 'n he'll wear out. Now it's not that us older folks are smarter than you youngsters, but at least we've had an opportunity to make most of the common mistakes. We've had our quota of disappointments and burned fingers. We've lost some of the fears and insecurities that plagued our youth. And, to the degree that we've learned from these experiences, we've gained some wisdom.*

The Generation Gap

Many employment dilemmas today are a result of a lack of respect and appreciation for intergenerational differences, says Rosemarin. And the misunderstandings work both ways.

One 58-year-old engineer displayed an attitude toward younger colleagues that a co-worker characterized as "Die, Yuppie scum." Because he showed his contempt so clearly, the engineer shouldn't have been surprised when his name showed up on his employer's list of job cuts. Then, when he had trouble finding another position, he blamed his problem on an indifferent job market. He might have had better luck if he had accepted responsibility for his own predicament and taken a more positive approach.

If you're interested in more traditional employment routes, be careful not to reinforce age-related stereotypes in interviews, says Rosemarin. Instead, take the initiative to show how (and why) you'll fit into the corporate culture. As a 50-something consultant, Rosemarin remembers working for a high-profile, youth-oriented entertainment company where anyone over 55 was considered ancient history. Rather than react defensively, she played up that she's a highly energetic woman who's always on the move with new ideas and projects—just like her creative clients. The recognition of similarities (age differences notwithstanding) made them much more receptive to the solutions she proposed.

Like comedian Rodney Dangerfield, some older workers are so busy complaining they "don't get no respect" that they fail to realize they aren't showing others much respect, either. Strangely enough, you can stop that cycle of disrespect by showing more self-respect. Once you know and appreciate your own value, no one can diminish your worth, no matter how rude they might be. What's more, when you present yourself as a self-respecting professional who's earned your wisdom and experience, others will be more inclined to treat you that way. In other words, the world might start to reflect back what you show it.

Rosemarin remembers her own astonishment when talking to a 29-year-old outplacement intern at Chemical Bank in New York who told her, "I can't wait to be your age." When pressed for reasons, the intern explained: "In this field, where I'm expected to counsel so many senior executives, age helps with credibility and respect." The intern's comment reinforced Rosemarin's belief that there are advantages to being whatever age you are. The real key is to recognize and promote those advantages. If you've achieved some stature in your field and want to continue achieving in leadership roles, this means building on your professional credentials rather than downplaying or denying them. You might be surprised to discover how much you can accomplish in the years you have left.

Limitless Potential

Many older adults don't recognize the depth and breadth of their own potential. Regardless of age, this can take some time, and experimentation with new life roles, to figure out.

The "Young-Old"

Benjamin Franklin was 70 years old when he was appointed to the committee that wrote the Declaration of Independence. When he was

72, he got France to recognize the United States. And, at 82, he worked with Congress to help ratify the Constitution.

Thomas Jefferson was 76 when he founded the University of Virginia.

At 67, George C. Marshall received the Nobel Prize for designing the European Recovery program after World War II.

Jessica Tandy was 79 when she won an Oscar for her portrayal of Daisy Werthan in *Driving Miss Daisy.* She was two years older when she was nominated again for her role as Ninny Threadgood in *Fried Green Tomatoes,* where she taught a much-younger Kathy Bates how to find joy in life.

Perhaps it's just an accident of fate or some extraordinary talent that led these go-getters to produce such memorable late-life accomplishments. However, it's hard not to note the myriad ways in which their attitudes toward life and aging inspired them to achieve. Instead of believing that there's some biological watershed when everything starts to deteriorate and go downhill, these productive adults worked in ways that kept them actively involved participants in the business of life. Each of these high achievers fit a category sociologist Bernice Neugarten called the "young-old." Rather than cave into some chronological divide, they parlayed their wisdom and experience into meaningful achievements that added years and dimensions to their lives. What they all had in common was a vision or a dream—an unwillingness to be held back by preconceptions, misconceptions, or fears.

At 45 years old, boxer George Foreman was more afraid of "not having a dream" than he was of climbing into the ring again with a much-younger opponent. The result was boxing history when he knocked out 26-year-old Michael Moorer in 1994 to regain the title he'd lost 20 years before and become the oldest heavyweight champion ever.

No Limits, No Finish Line

A former project engineer for a satellite communications company in New York City offered to help a widowed friend with her floundering restaurant. He thought he'd just be pitching in with salad-chopping or pancake-making (duties he had little experience with). However, his contribution turned out to be much bigger than that. Once he got a hands-on feel for the restaurant business, he found, to his surprise, that he knew how to do things he'd never realized he could. Before long, for example, he was helping improve the restaurant's layout, determine food requirements, and even plan the menu. All it took was applying the project-management skills and experience he'd already acquired in a different environment.

So, too, for Frank Mackey, whose entrepreneurial spirit and "tough hide" of self-confidence enabled him to break into the extremely competitive arena of commercial acting. While his younger colleagues lament the dearth of work, the 63-year-old Mackey religiously (and some would say relentlessly) makes his rounds to talent agents. In his very first six months of operation, Mackey has the beginnings of a portfolio that might make for a truly successful late-life career. Already, he's garnered projects with prestigious companies such as Sears, Roebuck and Company and Leo Burnett.

Some think he's crazy to have given up a lucrative legal career for the tough world of acting, where money and projects can be scarce and the focus is on youth and glamour. But, like the late Oscar Wilde, the upbeat Mackey believes, "The only thing you never regret in old age are your mistakes." He's looking forward to the future, not rehashing the errors of the past.

As a mature adult, it's time to start gauging for yourself what is and isn't "realistic" for you. Before caving into societal or peer pressure to accept a diminished (and unnecessarily unsatisfying) role in life, try approaching your life choices more creatively.

In *The Fifth Discipline* (1994, Doubleday), author Peter Senge questions whether we've become prisoners of "the system" or of our own limited way of thinking. He believes that a spirit of mastery (which goes beyond actual skill and competence) is the key to a creative and productive life. People with a high level of personal mastery live in a continual learning mode and consider the experience its own reward.

My colleague Steve Garrett, an independent outplacement consultant in Chicago, has a poster hanging on his living room wall that reads, "There is no finish line." At his annual holiday party, he caught me contemplating the poster with amusement.

"It's a reminder to enjoy the journey," he laughed. A moment of understanding passed between us. As outplacement professionals, we have seen too many people who are trying desperately to wait out their time until retirement. Collecting pension plans and retirement monies was once a feasible (and quite practical) workplace reality, but times have changed. Before you agree to turn your remaining work years into decades of drudgery, consider the importance of rich personal experience for lifelong happiness.

After 1,846 days and nights on the road—which included photo safaris in Kenya and Tanzania, voyages to Antarctica, cruises in the Baltic, and hiking in Ireland—Jack Schnedler, part-time travel editor for the *Chicago Sun-Times,* decided to give up his globetrotting life for a more settled existence as the managing editor of the *Arkansas Democrat-Gazette.* But he recognized the value of the memories he had built en route. "I can live comfortably on the interest I'll be drawing from these 12 years of indelibly banked travel editor's memories," he wrote in his last *Sun-Times* column.

The truth is, there is no finish line because there is no race. The only agenda that matters starts at birth and ends at death. As an act of self-empowerment, try abandoning the whole concept of retirement. Doing so can bring undreamed-of opportunities for growth and achievement. Too many people seem to accept the idea that work is automatically drudgery and leisure is more fulfilling. Yet many people's lives are enriched, rather than diminished, by their work. Viewing work as a way to meet your needs and enrich your life can be an emotionally rewarding experience.

"That's the beauty of it," says Anita Lands. "There is no right or wrong answer. It's all up to you."

Tips for Saving for Early Retirement

Savings are usually the key to an early retirement, even if you have a generous pension. If your savings fall short, there are three ways you can still get on track for an early out.

Step 1: Save smart. Take full advantage of any 401(k) or 403(b) or other employer-sponsored tax-deferred retirement plans. No other investment vehicles can give you the triple whammy of regular savings, tax-deferred compounding, and employer-matched funding. If you contribute as much as your plan allows and invest wisely, you could end up with a higher benefit in retirement than someone with a traditional pension plan. At the very least, contribute enough to earn the full employer match. Then stretch your budget so that you can save as much as the plan allows.

Step 2: Make saving painless. If you change jobs, arrange for your employer to transfer your retirement-plan balance directly to your new employer's plan or a rollover IRA. When you get a raise, increase your 401(k) salary-deferral rate if possible, or have automatic monthly deposits made into a separate savings fund.

Step 3: Be aggressive. Make your money work as hard as you do. Diversify your investments. Most people play it too safe with their retirement savings, especially in the early years of a long-term investment.

Source: Adapted from *Kiplinger's Personal Finance* magazine.

Oh No, 50!: Midlife Career Transitions Thought-Starter Worksheet

1. How old are you now?

   ____

2. How much longer do you plan to work?

   ____

3. Are you looking forward to retirement? Or do you dread it?

   ____

   ____

4. Do you know what you want to do after you retire?

   ____

   ____

5. Do you plan/need to work after retirement?

   ____

6. If you plan to work, do you know what you want to do?

   ____

   ____

7. Is there anything you need to do now to make sure you can do what you want after retirement?

   ____

   ____

   ____

8. What is your stereotype of an "old person"?

   ____

   ____

9. How do you plan to combat that reality?

____

____

____

10. How healthy are you?

____

11. Is there anything you can do now to take better care of your health?

____

____

____

12. Are you open to learning new things? Why or why not?

____

____

____

13. When was the last time you tried something totally different? How did it feel?

____

____

____

14. How well do you function in an unstructured environment?

____

____

(continues)

(continued)

15. How do you plan to structure your time after retirement?

____

____

____

____

16. Do you have friends who plan to retire when you do?

____

17. If you don't have friends retiring with you, where do you expect to find community?

____

____

18. Is it important to you to feel like a productive, contributing member of society? How do you plan to fulfill that need after retirement?

____

____

____

____

19. Have you ever participated in any volunteer or community activities? What was that experience like?

____

____

____

20. Do you have a formal retirement plan?

____

21. Have you considered working with a retirement-planning counselor to create one? If not, why?

____

____

____

22. Do you have any creative instincts? If so, how do you plan to fulfill them?

____

____

____

____

23. Will you need extra income after retirement?

____

____

24. Are there any skills or experience you should be getting now to ensure your marketability later?

____

____

____

____

25. Is there anyone over age 65 whom you really admire?

____

26. Why do you admire this person?

____

____

____

(continues)

(continued)

27. Is there anything in this person's attitude or behavior that you can work to emulate?

____

____

____

28. How long do you plan to live?

____

29. How are you going to make your later years fulfilling?

____

____

____

____

PART 2

Career Security

CHAPTER 5

Achieving Career Security in Turbulent Times

Security no longer comes from being employed...it must come from being employable.

—Rosabeth Moss Kanter, *When Giants Learn to Dance*

Only an ostrich that's had its head buried in the sand for the past two decades could be unaware of the massive downsizing that has been rocking the American workplace. Odds are you—or someone you know—has already been affected. And even if you know you're in good company, being a layoff victim is a pretty traumatic experience, especially because the rules of job hunting have changed. Gone are the days when you could expect to fill out an application one week and be on the job the next. In this increasingly competitive market, you have to work hard just to get someone to read your resume (and it's a miracle of miracles if they actually ask to meet with you). Interviews might include five managers instead of one, and it might take a year to land a new position where it used to take a month.

If you've been lucky so far, don't count on avoiding the ax forever. The days of cradle-to-grave employment are over. Never again will anyone guarantee you a paycheck for life. The only way to enjoy true career security today is to build yourself a network of contacts, some financial reserves, and a set of marketable skills. And you shouldn't wait until the last minute to do so because none of these tools can be thrown together overnight.

However, if you recently lost your job and weren't prepared for it, don't lose hope. It's too easy to start conjuring up worst-case scenarios when you're unemployed:

> *I'll have to sell the house and move into a smaller place. The kids won't have enough money to pay for college. They'll have to take out huge loans or stay home. My spouse will have to go back to work or take a second job. I'll end up doing manual labor for entry-level wages.*
>
> *Then, my family will leave me and I'll end up on welfare. I'll have to start living out of my car, or move into a homeless shelter. Soon, I'll become a skid-row derelict drinking my dinner from a bottle. I'll end up just like that desperate guy in the suit who was standing at the expressway entrance the other day—the one with the sandwich board that read: "I'll take any job for $20,000 a year."*

Such disaster fantasies won't make you feel better and won't help you out of a bad employment situation. What you need is a whole new mind-set and an action plan to sustain your career. This chapter gives the details on the actions I suggest.

Do Good Work

A first-rate engineer with an impressive education and strong professional credentials always met—or exceeded—his employer's standards for excellence. His company, a health-care-equipment manufacturer in Niles, Illinois, consistently rewarded his achievements with raises, promotions, and challenging new assignments. So, when a two-year plan was announced to dismantle the manufacturing plant he called home, the engineer didn't worry. He assumed they'd need him to help close down the place and then move him into another division.

He was wrong. Within six weeks of the announcement, his name showed up on the very first list of job cuts. It wasn't personal, and he knew it. It was a straight business decision. His forte was improving the quality of the plant's manufacturing process. That talent was completely unnecessary after the company decided to shut the plant. Hence, he got his walking papers.

If a great performance record doesn't guarantee you a place on the payroll, what's the point of trying to do a good job?

- Because you'll feel better about yourself if you have to enter the job market. You'll know that the exigencies of business forced you out, not lackadaisical performance on your part.
- Because it will improve your marketable skills, even if you can't use them with your current employer.
- Because it will remind others that it's a pleasure to work with you. Then, if you're laid off, co-workers are more likely to help you find something else. In other words, it will cement your network.
- And finally, because it will encourage your employer to find you another job within the organization if the company decides to downsize.

In the engineer's case, that's exactly what happened. Even though he was among the first to be "redeployed," he landed another position within the same company before his 60-day notice expired.

Develop Marketable Skills

Benjamin Barber, a political science professor at Rutgers University, once commented that the world could be divided into two categories: learners and nonlearners. Under the rules of the new employment game, learners will be clear winners. The engineer who was redeployed clearly is a learner. It helps that his work creates continuous opportunities for him to acquire and practice new skills. As a quality-control expert with state-of-the-art knowledge, he's developed competencies that his employer knows would be tough to duplicate.

Your job might not have that kind of challenge built into its daily routine. Rather than lament your fate, try seeking out formal training or volunteering for company projects that will allow you to enhance your skill set.

For a 45-year-old plant manager with a suburban Chicago food manufacturer, this meant taking the time and initiative to enroll in an evening MBA program. It wasn't always fun. He hadn't set foot in a classroom in 25 years, and there were plenty of nights when he didn't feel like studying or sitting in class after a hard day at work. Other days, he truly enjoyed the learning environment. It got his creative juices flowing again, which hadn't happened at the plant for a long, long time.

The manager had begun his master's work because he knew he couldn't afford to let his skills become obsolete. As it turns out, his advance planning paid off. Three years into the program, his company went through (yet another) reorganization. Offered an early-retirement package, the plant manager took the money and ran. He used part of his severance package for tuition and completed his degree within a year. Then he decided to embark on a new career in marketing. Some people think he should've stayed with his old job because it was never directly threatened. But he has no regrets. "The package was a sure thing," he says. "My future there wasn't, considering the way the company is headed. I feel better for taking the initiative instead of waiting for the next round of cuts. It's the best thing I ever did. Now I can get on with my life."

Management guru Tom Peters would undoubtedly applaud this man's strategy. Peters argues that we now live in a brain-based economy where "education is economics and economics is education." The key to winning, he says, is to get and stay one step smarter than the next person—to make a commitment to "school for life." He echoes the sentiments of H.G. Wells, who once said, "The story of human survival is a race between education and catastrophe."

Formal schooling isn't the only way to expand your knowledge and expertise, however. Experience is also a great teacher. Organizations in flux offer endless opportunities for on-the-job learning. Too many people who work at such firms waste valuable time nursing their wounds and griping about their employers. It's far wiser to contribute your talents wherever the company needs them. That way, you earn a reputation as a team player and gain valuable skills.

Be Willing to Pitch In

A personnel coordinator who aspired to human resource management saw her career track fizzle following a downsizing. After 14 years with a suburban L.A.–based food manufacturer, she was forced to accept a demotion. Her new role as an inventory control clerk taxed her patience more than her brainpower.

Determined to make the most of a less-than-perfect situation, she set about trying to improve her qualifications and her standing with the company. To do so, she volunteered to produce a newsletter for the company's total-quality-management initiative. This activity kept her from getting bored and increased her visibility in the company.

She also improved her status with her boss by positioning herself to assume his supervisory responsibilities when he couldn't be in the office. Taken together, these two steps kept her involved and growing for almost a year. But, as often happens in the real world, her diligence wasn't rewarded with either a promotion or a raise. Still, she had the comfort of knowing that she'd developed a more marketable set of skills and could easily move elsewhere.

Expect the Unexpected

If you're security-conscious, you probably like your work life orderly and predictable. Good luck. Ironically, the people most likely to keep their jobs these days are those who can operate comfortably in chaos. These professionals show the range and flexibility to do whatever is required. You can't be all things to all people. You might, however, be able to stretch yourself more than you realize and learn to enjoy the satisfactions that stem from overcoming a challenge. You'll soon feel more secure knowing that you can manage organizational changes rather than cave into them.

I was personally gratified to witness this transformation in one of my more resistant outplacement clients. A 42-year-old tax administrator, she'd spent her entire adult work life in the same department of the same Chicago bank. She liked her job, her boss, and the bank. But most of all, she liked her routine and would've been perfectly content to spend the rest of her career right where she was.

You can probably guess the next part of the story. One morning, she arrived at work to learn the bank had decided to outsource its trust department to an accounting firm. Suddenly, there were a dozen unanchored tax pros roaming the bank's corridors in search of new jobs.

My client was a totally reliable employee, but she was also painfully shy. Despite her long years of service, she knew only a handful of her co-workers. When I told her that she needed to "network" with other bank employees to get resituated, she balked. In fact, my advice so upset her that she complained to her manager about me. But I don't make the rules. It wasn't my idea to make networking the number-one way people find jobs. I just pass the information along and try to help people become as effective at that process as possible.

Fortunately, she finally got the message and, with her manager's support, arranged an informational interview the very same day. She came back from that meeting a changed woman. Apparently, the person she met with had been so nice and supportive that she wondered why she'd ever objected to the process! Less than one week later, she landed another position within the bank that was suitable to her temperament and skills. In fact, she was the first person in her department to be rehired. She never thanked me for pushing her to network. But when she came to say goodbye, I could see she was truly delighted at her success and pleased with her new opportunity. As she left, I had to laugh when she remarked, "I know I should do more networking. But right now, I'd really like to take this new job."

Develop an Innovative Spirit

Because employers are always seeking a competitive edge, they love having innovators on staff. Such professionals are seldom content with the status quo, so they're constantly on the lookout for new ways to improve conditions. They also tend to turn an analytical and creative eye toward problems.

Consider Kathy Reed, who realized early in her career that being a stockbroker didn't suit her. According to an article in the *Wall Street Journal,* she longed to work for Xerox, but the company's Dallas facility wouldn't even hire her as a secretary. Undeterred, she called a local temporary agency and said she'd only accept assignments at Xerox. Within weeks, she landed a temp assignment there, and was soon offered a full-time secretarial position that allowed her to network her way up from the inside.

Try to show creativity in your employment searches and on the job. If you devise a way to save your company money, improve customer relations, or develop a new revenue stream, you can be sure that you're more than earning your keep. This doesn't mean that your job will necessarily be spared when the ax falls. However, it will guarantee you a more impressive resume and a great set of problem-solving skills.

Having good problem-solving skills should do a lot to enhance your peace of mind. After all, what is a job search if not a problem to be solved?

Learn to Manage Risk

It's natural to want to feel comfortable and safe. But such an attitude can be hazardous in a technology-driven society where standing still often means falling behind.

Helen Keller once said, "Security is mostly a superstition....Avoiding danger is no safer in the long run than outright exposure. Life is either a daring adventure or nothing." Keller, as we all know, overcame some of the most devastating barriers imaginable to achieve great things in the world. Compared with her inspirational example, it's shameful how wimpy and risk-averse so many of us have become. It might be scary to take some calculated risk with your future, but you might also be surprised by the zest it adds to your work life.

A 25-year veteran of the Bell System learned this lesson well. Fresh out of engineering school at 22, he'd joined forces with the phone company as a field engineer in Chicago and stayed...and stayed...and stayed. Like many corporate Goliaths, the Bell System was once a bastion of stability where "lifers" traded a career's worth of devoted service for guaranteed employment.

No more. After divestiture, he was declared "surplus" or "at risk" on three different occasions. He always managed to save himself at the eleventh hour, but the uncertainty took an emotional toll.

"I was clinging to my employer like a prisoner to his jail bars," he says. At age 47, he was eight years short of a full pension and, if he could help it, he wasn't going anywhere without it. But eight years is a long time to spend hanging onto the edge of a lifeboat. He didn't make it. Right after his 50th birthday, the company offered him a new package that made leaving more palatable. It cost him 25 percent of his pension to walk away. But, at his age, he figured it was a better alternative than staying. He no longer wanted to spend precious time passively waiting to leave—especially because there was no guarantee he could last another five years.

"Ten years ago, it would have been heresy to say you wanted to leave Bell," he says. "Today, it's idiotic for someone like me to stay." It helped that he'd built a strong financial safety net through his 25 years of service. "If I didn't take the risk, I knew that I'd always regret the missed opportunity," he says. "That seemed like a bigger risk than not trying."

Once free, he gambled again—this time on a franchise operation. Last I heard from him, he and his two teenagers were happily dishing out yogurt to health-conscious customers.

Risky? Perhaps. But because risk is inevitable, at least you can choose the kinds of chances you want to take. This Bell veteran loves the newfound feeling that he has more control over his own destiny.

For the 45-and-over crowd, age might be the greatest deterrent to risk-taking. With seemingly little margin for error, the consequences of making a mistake loom larger. Yet in reality, there might be as much risk in staying put as there is in leaving familiar ground. Expert job-hunting skills can minimize some of the anxiety that comes from taking more employment chances.

Know How to Job Hunt

My friend's apartment building has a new doorman. You can tell by his attitude that he thinks he's too good for the job.

Actually, he's one of the worst doormen I ever met. He always makes it clear when he opens the door that he's doing you a favor. Personally, I'd rather open the door myself than deal with his condescending attitude. Once he told me that he likes to punish tenants who aren't nice to him. Unless they smile and say "Good morning," he won't open the door.

He makes a point of telling people that he's not a doorman by choice. He's an engineer who's stuck opening doors for people until he finds another real engineering job (I hope he finds one soon so the rest of us won't have to suffer through his attitude much longer).

For some reason, this guy brings out the worst in me. I know I should be more sympathetic to his plight: After all, I'm a career-development expert and this guy needs his career back big time. But he doesn't make me want to help him. Nor am I alone. My friend doesn't like him, either, and thinks he's rude.

Actually, when I first heard about his situation, I felt sorry for him and offered to look over his resume. He rebuffed me. He's sent out more than 300 resumes (and barely gotten any response), but he's convinced the problem is his age and not his resume. Nobody wants a 53-year-old engineer, he says.

Before you decry his victimization, however, I ask you to consider other possible reasons for his dilemma.

First, his job search lacks meaningful focus. While he did make up a list of potential employers and send out a "broadcast letter" announcing his availability, he didn't take the extra step it takes to make that strategy productive. He needs to know more about each company's specific goals and explain in letters or networking interviews how he might be able to add value.

For example, he's multilingual. With a little extra effort, he could identify companies that are doing (or planning to do) business in Germany. At such firms, his German language skills could be useful.

Also, he doesn't individualize his letters in any way. He doesn't bother to figure out which division of a company to target or who the likely hiring managers would be. He just shoots off a letter to anonymous personnel managers saying, "I need a job." Nor does he follow up his correspondence with telephone calls to make sure it's been received and read. He never makes it clear to employers that he's a real-live person with a valuable contribution to make to an organization.

Worst of all, this engineer-turned-doorman is ignoring the cardinal rule of job hunting: Network, network, network. Any job-search book will tell you that at least three-quarters of all positions are filled through networking or word-of-mouth. A candidate without a networking strategy eliminates 75 percent to 85 percent of potential employment opportunities a priori. That's ignorance or stubbornness, not age discrimination.

The truth is, this man's attitude is his biggest problem. He seems to think the world owes him a living, and he's mad at the people who are giving him one for making him earn it. All the networking in the world won't help if you turn potential contacts off with a sour-grapes disposition.

I don't care what age you are, this engineer's search strategy won't work for any professional these days. Like it or not, you simply have to go the extra mile to attract employers' interest today.

Savvy careerists know how to market themselves in an entrepreneurial way. They take stock of their marketable skills, research and identify employers who need those talents, and make every effort to let them know that (1) they want to work for the firm, and (2) they have something unique to offer.

Like it or not, the rules have changed. You can get with the program or get left out in the cold. Your choice.

You have to educate yourself for success in this employment market. If job hunting is unfamiliar territory, make the bookstore or library your first stop. Hundreds of books have been written that can help you improve your search skills.

There's also a burgeoning field of career and outplacement counselors who coach people on how to find jobs. If you get your walking papers, knowing how to access those resources and learn about the process is key to finding a new job.

Feed Your Rolodex

We all know the cliché: "It's who you know that counts." But if you aren't very good at networking, you won't want to believe it's true. Actually, it's even more complicated than that.

"How about this for higher math?" asks management guru and author Tom Peters. "Security is proportional to (1) the thickness of your Rolodex; (2) the rate of Rolodex expansion; (3) the share of Rolodex entries from beyond the corporate walls; and (4) the time devoted to Rolodex maintenance."

Let me try to explain Peters' "art of Rolodexing":

- *The thickness of your Rolodex* refers to the sheer number of people that you know—the more the better. Because no one's job is safe anymore, it's wise not to depend too much on any one person for your future. Cultivating a broad network of people who know and appreciate your work is one of the best forms of security you can create in this job market.
- *The rate of Rolodex expansion* implies that you should never feel you know enough people. New and important players are emerging in every field and industry all the time. If you want to know where the growth and opportunities are, you need to constantly add new contacts to your network—preferably before you ever want or need anything from them.
- *The share of Rolodex entries from beyond the corporate walls* means that having a diverse group of friends and acquaintances is also critical. If your network consists only of co-workers, you'll be in trouble if your company ever goes belly-up. Try to meet professionals who work in other parts of your industry and/or those who have similar functions in other industries.

  Remember the quality engineer I mentioned earlier in this chapter? His job brought him into contact with many people both inside and outside his company. These colleagues liked him and respected his work. So, as soon as he learned his job was being eliminated, he thumbed through his phone directory and called crucial contacts to let them know what was happening. Vendors proved extremely helpful. Because they were out in the world soliciting business from competitors, they were able to provide him with a wealth of information and contacts. If you have a more isolated job, you can expand your horizons by participating actively in professional and trade associations.
- *The time devoted to Rolodex maintenance.* You know the drill: out of sight, out of mind. If you don't keep up with your contacts,

Warning Signs That Your Job Might Be in Jeopardy

1. Your boss has started treating you differently—but definitely not better. Your efforts don't seem to be recognized or appreciated.
2. Ditto for your subordinates, who have started to go around you (or over your head) when they have a complaint or need direction or information.
3. You have a new boss who seems intent on finding fault with you.
4. Your boss has a new boss.
5. Your job is getting too big for one person to handle. It's a setup for you to fail.
6. Your job is getting smaller, and soon they may not need you at all.
7. Your budget, expenses, and perks are getting slashed. The company may be hoping you'll get overstressed and burn out.
8. Your performance ratings are slipping, but you know your work has been fine. This is a surefire sign that the hand of office politics is operating.
9. The company is going through a restructuring.
10. Your company has been acquired or merged.

they forget about you. Staying in touch takes some extra daily effort, but smart careerists do it.

Once a week or so, I get a call from some colleague I haven't seen in a while. Typically, the person just wants to find out what's new with me or update me with some change in his or her situation. Sometimes, the caller shares an interesting bit of industry gossip. I appreciate this kind of initiative. No one makes it completely alone. It's good to be included in the circle of Information—to know what's happening.

While networking requires a higher level of social alertness and more concentrated energy, it doesn't have to be drudgery. You just need to find ways to make it enjoyable. Try pairing it up with another activity like going to church, attending a lecture, or playing on a softball team. Shared activities make for shared friendships, and friends make pleasant networking partners.

Some of it will still feel like work, particularly if your strategy includes returning to school for more education or taking on new responsibilities for which you're not getting paid. Still, the effort will be worth it. Just remember that desperate man who has to resort to wearing a sandwich board that announces his bottom-line price. Where are his friends and contacts now? Where are the people who know his work and appreciate it? Why is he forced to announce his plight to a million harried commuters?

Or consider the doorman who makes himself believe that his age is his problem and not his personality. Is this an attitude that would make you feel better about yourself?

Think about it: Wouldn't you rather be eating dinner with colleagues at a monthly meeting of your professional association? Wouldn't you rather be building both competence and goodwill? Or would you rather wait and take your chances on the "kindness of strangers"?

It's been nearly 40 years since William Whyte wrote his classic, *The Organization Man* (1956, Simon & Schuster), in which he warned that rigid hierarchical corporate structures would stifle initiative and breed stultifying conformity.

If you've lived in that world a long time, you may find it hard to accept that it's a whole new ballgame now. For organizations, and the people who staff and manage them, the only real security lies in the ability to grow, change, and adapt. You can fight this new reality. Or you can celebrate your liberation.

Achieving Career Security in Turbulent Times Thought-Starter Worksheet

1. On a scale of 1 to 10, with 1 being least secure and 10 most secure, how secure is your job?

7

2. Is your job more secure or less secure than it was five years ago? Ten years ago? Last year?

less and more

3. Looking toward the future, do you think you'll still have your job next year? Five years from now? Ten years from now?

Next year

4. If your job security is diminishing, what can you do to make yourself feel more secure?

Acquire more skills

5. Do you have an aggressive investment strategy?

No

6. If you don't have a good investment strategy, have you consulted with a financial planner?

No

(continues)

(continued)

7. Do you consider yourself marketable?

Yes

8. If your skills aren't marketable, what can you do (or are you currently doing) to upgrade them?

9. Do you think you're too old to go to school? If so, why?

No

10. Do you fear age discrimination?

No

11. Which of the following "age-discrimination fighters" should be part of your plan:

- ❑ Dyeing your hair?
- ❑ Increasing your energy with exercise and healthy eating?
- ☑ Updating your skills?
- ☑ Fixing your attitude?
- ☑ Networking with friends?
- ☑ Expanding your network?
- ☑ Perfecting your job search skills?

12. Do you know how to conduct an effective job search?

Not really

13. If your resume is outdated, can you start revising it now?

✓

14. How strong is your network?

✓

15. If your network is too limited, how can you begin to expand your contact base now?

Talk to everyone I know

16. Does self-employment interest you?

Yes

17. What do you see as the obstacles to self-employment?

$ $

experience

18. Have you asked others who have made the transition to self-employment how they accomplished their goals? If not, why not?

Don't know anyone.

19. Do you consider yourself employable?

Yes

(continues)

(continued)

20. What can you do now to improve your employability?

____

____

____

21. Do you consider yourself an aggressive person?

______________________ NO ______________________

22. Are you being too passive about your future?

______________________ NO ______________________

CHAPTER 6

How to Love the Job You Hate

Labor without joy is base.

—**John Ruskin**

In the Disney classic, *Snow White and the Seven Dwarfs*, Snow White is a hard-working girl with too much to do. But this didn't stop her—and her forest animal friends—from whistling while they worked. In the process, they became role models (of sorts) for a generation of Americans.

Unfortunately, most of us prefer to grumble and be unhappy. (One survey found that four out of five working Americans were dissatisfied with their jobs.) It's a misery that knows no boundaries. No age, race, or group is exempt. It doesn't matter if you're a college graduate or a high school dropout. A man or a woman. A doctor, a manager, or a grocery-store clerk. Too many employees aren't having much fun.

But whether your complaint is a bad boss, too much bureaucracy, office politics, boring work, or all of the above, you don't have to suffer in silence (or not so silently). You can take steps to improve your situation, even if you can't afford to leave. Once you begin intervening on your own behalf, you'll start feeling less like a victim of circumstance and more like a professional with influence and control over your own destiny. The following strategies should help move your thinking in the right direction.

Strategy 1: Stop Watching the Clock

The hands on the clock tend to move more slowly when you watch them. Boredom is stultifying. Rather than kill time and wait for the day to end, your challenge is to find ways to get more involved—to enlarge your job without merely adding more work. The key is to think qualitatively, not quantitatively. Not more, but better.

How? For starters, keep your eyes and ears open for new projects that interest you. Or, better yet, invent a project that solves an organizational problem and gets your juices going.

A retail store manager used her company's national sales meeting to get a better handle on what was going on throughout the company. Because her interests were advertising and marketing, she focused extra attention on talking with people from those departments to learn more about their needs and goals. When she learned they wanted to investigate the home shopping market, she volunteered to do the research. This gave her a chance to study an interesting new trend, demonstrate her creativity and initiative, showcase her research and writing skills, and establish contacts with the right people. And, should the company decide to move ahead with the idea, she's also positioned herself to be a part of it.

This required the manager to do some extra work. But because she hopes to use the new knowledge to make a job change within the company, she considers the effort worth it. Some doors might now open that were previously closed.

In general, try to take a synergistic approach that involves other people in healthy and productive ways, recommends psychologist Laurie Anderson in Oak Park, Illinois. For example, if you need to free up your schedule to make room for new duties, try delegating tedious responsibilities to an employee who'd appreciate them.

"What's boring to you may be developmental to someone else," Anderson says. "Try looking for someone in the organization who'd like to learn the things that no longer interest you."

Anderson tells the story of a staffing professional who was burned out on recruitment and a trainer who'd overdosed on training. The two split their jobs in half and traded responsibilities so that both could enjoy new growth. The staffing professional was surprised to find how much she liked training. In fact, she liked it so much that she decided to become a trainer full time—a career direction she'd never anticipated.

Developing creative, synergistic solutions not only moves you out of a stuck position, it also enables you to build stronger alliances through shared responsibilities.

Strategy 2: Learn to Take a Compliment

It always feels good to know that you and the work you do are appreciated by others. Unfortunately, compliments tend to be few and far between, whereas criticism is never in short supply.

Why is there such a discrepancy? A president of a well-known commercial bank notes, "Every time I tell someone they're doing a good job, they ask me for more money. Then they end up getting mad when I tell them I can't give them a raise right now."

The president is caught in a classic Catch-22. No matter what he does, he'll be the bad guy—either for not noticing and praising employees' work or for praising it without simultaneously reaching into the company coffers for more funds. Unless he starts handing out raises and bonuses along with his compliments, he can't win.

The same no-win situation tends to surround performance appraisals. Many managers are reluctant to overpraise their subordinates because of the money demands that inevitably follow. As one shipping supervisor complained, "If I'm doing such a great job, how come I only got a three-percent raise?"

There are two sides to every story. Managers should praise people for a job well done, even if they aren't planning to follow up with financial rewards. Meanwhile, employees should learn how to accept compliments for what they are: a show of appreciation.

Unhook the compliment from the salary demand so that you can feel good about the praise rather than angry about the money. As a professional, you can't think like an hourly employee who gets something extra for every bit of extra effort. That was a hard line to draw for a successful litigation attorney who left the "fast track" for the "mommy track" when her third child was born.

As a partner, she'd shared equity in the firm's profits. On the mommy track, she remained a partner in name, but was paid an hourly consulting fee instead. In the sixth year of that arrangement, she took on a big case that demanded more than her usual three-day workweek. She pitched in willingly because her kids were in school all day, and achieved an outstanding result.

Her partners were so thrilled, they celebrated with a champagne lunch, toasted her accomplishments, and praised her abilities to the skies. Within weeks of the verdict, she decided to renegotiate her deal. If she was going to work as hard as the partners, she wanted her equity partnership reinstated. The partners listened, acknowledged her accomplishment, and questioned whether she was ready to commit once again to a full-time partnership. When she balked, they balked. Finally, they compromised by increasing her hourly consulting fee. Although better than nothing, the outcome didn't please her. "What's the point of knocking myself out for these guys, when no one appreciates my contribution?" she grumbled.

After this response, you can be sure the partners won't be so lavish with their praise next time around.

Strategy 3: Pat Yourself on the Back (Occasionally)

Perhaps you'd consider it a luxury to have someone at work say, "Thank you. Good job," once in a while. If so, you're not alone.

Many people feel their work is taken for granted. Certainly, colleagues and bosses can be competitive, and some customers are a royal pain in the you-know-where. But although those people might not be handing out recognition awards on your behalf, you can still feel good about yourself if you recognize and acknowledge your own strengths and achievements.

Despite the common complaint that egotistical braggarts with inflated notions of their own potential fill the workforce, the reverse is often true. Personally, I've seen hundreds of self-critical people who constantly undervalue their own abilities and sell themselves short. Because they're so hard on themselves, they need more praise and approval from others than often is forthcoming. The result, inevitably, is some kind of hostile dependency on the person (often a boss) perceived to be withholding. In fact, however, the problem is that the person is withholding praise from him- or herself.

To get out of such a rut, one competent trainer realized she needed a more objective way to evaluate her own capabilities. So she'd read and reread her seminar evaluations from customers, in which she was routinely praised for her patience, good humor, and informative style. Whenever she felt bad about herself, the evaluations would remind her that she truly was a good and competent person.

Another demoralized marketing manager (who was relegated to the gulags during a corporate reorganization) put her abilities in perspective by compiling a portfolio that showcased her greatest achievements. She included newspaper articles describing some of her more successful ventures, and some glowing letters of recommendation from managers and colleagues. Then, she consolidated that information into an impressive resume. Although she knew it might be a year or more before she'd actively job hunt, putting those documents together was very reparative. Whenever she felt isolated in her role, she used the material as a professional mirror that reflected her real skills and accomplishments.

Other professionals call attention to their successes through internal memos and letters. A savvy public relations professional wrote thank-you notes to everyone who'd helped him accomplish his publicity goals, and sent copies of the letters to his manager. Although this strategy took time out from an already busy calendar, it made everyone who worked with him feel good about their contributions while highlighting the PR man's leadership and organizational skills. While patting others on the back, he was subtly praising himself as well—a tactic you could call "enlightened self-interest."

Strategy 4: Take Criticism for What It's Worth

Just because someone says you're a bad person doesn't mean you're a jerk. It just means that someone doesn't like you. Although being disliked might be painful to tolerate, it's not a reflection of your self-worth. Personality conflicts make for hostile confrontations that are hurtful to everyone involved. Worse, the insults that get hurled at you tend to linger in your mind for years.

A 30-year-old journalist still remembers how humiliated she felt when a manager called her "immature and childish"—even though she was only 23 at the time. To this day, whenever she recalls the incident, the remark brings tears to her eyes and she lashes out in fury.

Recognize a battle of egos for what it is—unhealthy competition—and try, if possible, to recast the controversy into more neutral and professional waters. For example, a computer programmer who was told he was a snob asked for specific examples of incidents when he'd intentionally made his accuser feel inferior. After hearing one example, the programmer realized that a gesture of distaste he'd made about an assignment had been misconstrued by his co-worker as a personal insult. Once the misunderstanding was cleared up, the two felt much less resentful of each other. Asking for specific examples of your supposedly noxious behavior can help you gain insight into the true nature of the criticism that's been leveled at you—as long as you're truly open to what the data means.

Most people don't know how to give constructive criticism or receive it. In general, the more you respect others' talents and feelings, the more likely you'll be to couch your criticism in useful language. On the other side of the table, the more confident and self-aware you are, the more likely you'll be able to hear and evaluate the criticism fairly.

To become more effective at handling criticism constructively, keep the following guidelines in mind:

- Don't assume the other person is right or wrong. Obtain more than one point of view to determine its accuracy.
- Try not to be defensive. Ask yourself: Is there any truth to what this person is saying?
- Accept responsibility for fixing what needs fixing.
- Even if your feelings are hurt, don't harbor a grudge against the giver. It will only poison your relationship.

Strategy 5: View Politics as a Challenge

The worst workplace atrocities take place in the name of "office politics." Usually, the term is applied to the ugly underbelly of group life. It refers to the manipulative and mean-spirited ways people backstab or "kiss up to" each other in the effort to get ahead.

Office politics can make for rotten bedfellows: greedy, conniving, manipulative bedfellows. And if you're like many, you don't want anything to do with that nasty scene. You'd rather sit in the corner of the lunchroom alone with your nose buried in the newspaper. Or stay in your office with the door closed, burrowed in a stack of reports and memos.

You can hide behind the mountains of paperwork on your desk, but there's nowhere to go. You're trapped. While others are gossiping at the water cooler or walking arm-in-arm to the local bar (deeply engrossed in conversation), you're turning into a sullen, isolated person who's always the last to learn about things you need to know.

Invisibility has its price. People know you sit in judgment of them and, guess what, they're not going to let *you* get in the way of *their* goals. What's more, you can't achieve success entirely on your own. Sure, Paul Simon wanted to believe, "I am a rock. I am an island." But did you happen to notice Art Garfunkel on backup making him look good?

The term "office politics" has such a bad connotation that you might well forget it altogether. Because it's good for your career to get along with co-workers, why not call it "social intelligence" instead? Start viewing "politics" as the developmental challenge of getting along with difficult people.

"Most people aren't political enough," says Mike Murphy of the Signet Group, an outplacement firm in Chicago. "They want to bury their heads in the sand and hope the problem will go away. They don't realize you can't solve a problem by ignoring it."

Using a Conflict to Get Ahead

Two senior managers had trouble getting along, which was creating problems for their subordinates as well as the VP who supervised them. In a particularly astute political move, one manager decided to find ways to relate better to her (more volatile) colleague. She shared this goal with the VP, and together they brainstormed the possibilities.

By demonstrating the initiative to solve the problem and further her boss's agenda, this savvy manager turned an interpersonal conflict into an opportunity to improve her team-playing skills and strengthen her alliance with higher-ups. Meanwhile, the other manager began looking like a difficult, irrational person to work with.

For the manager who made the extra effort, there are two immediate payoffs. First, she's no longer a passive victim of her co-worker's moodiness. Second, her boss is now more likely to cooperate with her when incidents arise. There are long-term benefits, too. Down the road, she's likely to be viewed (and to view herself) as a team player who keeps her cool under pressure. Of the two, who would *you* recommend for a promotion?

The moral of the story: The next time some irrational but highly ambitious co-worker gets under your skin, experiment with creative ways to use the experience to your professional advantage. In other words, find a way to get even by getting ahead. Although this can be a real test of interpersonal skill, it's worth the effort. When office animosities run high, careers get sabotaged. Hostilities escalate. And you can end up dreading every minute in the office.

As long as you're committed to staying, you'll have to find a way to fit in with the people you must work with. I'm not talking best buddies here—just cordial working relationships. The alliances you form should enhance your career goals and satisfaction; otherwise, there's no point in forming them. Rather than lament the politics, you need a rational strategy for working with difficult people. Ranting and raving won't work. Neither will silent suffering ("poor me" makes you look more pitiful than powerful). Is it really so gratifying to play the victim? Wouldn't you rather try a stronger, more assertive role?

Reaching Out

A sales representative for an office-equipment company hated the all-male team on which she was expected to play. She considered her co-workers loud, crass, and ignorant. She wanted no part of what she considered their "male posturing" and was determined to "put them in their place."

For her, it was both feminist pride and personal preference. Rather than join into what she called their "macho boys club," she refused all invitations to lunch or after-work drinks, telling her husband: "I'd rather eat lunch with a pig. You have no idea how gross those guys are."

It didn't take long for her co-workers to get the message. They might have been gross, but they weren't stupid. To say she didn't "fit in" would be putting her case mildly. It was almost as if she didn't work there. During weekly staff meetings, all conversation would stop when she walked into the room. There were lots of occasional glances in her direction, but no one ever addressed her directly. And, when she did speak up, her comments would be met with complete silence. It was eerie and intimidating.

Yet she was an excellent sales rep and, much to her surprise, she had been turning in the best sales performance of her life. Her husband suspected that her desire to show her coworkers up was behind the achievement. When word got out, funny things started to happen. A decision was made, for example, to reorganize sales territories. When the new assignments were handed out, she saw immediately that she had a smaller piece of the pie. When she complained to her sales manager, she was told: "You're not a team player. The better territories are reserved for the team players." She protested vehemently. Obviously, she'd already proved that she could handle a larger region. She'd earned and deserved a better assignment, not a smaller one.

The manager was firm: "This is a company that values team play. We don't want to send a message that we value individual effort more than the group. You have to learn how to play on the team."

Rather than leave (which she surely would've been justified in doing), the sales rep decided to become more involved with her group. After all, she reasoned, there are going to be politics everywhere. How did she do it? She didn't turn herself into a cheerleader overnight—or ever. That would've been too much. Instead, she singled out the person who'd taken over a piece of her territory and made a goodwill gesture by inviting him to lunch to discuss some of the accounts. He looked surprised, but agreed. During the meeting, she was sincere and helpful. He seemed to appreciate her comments.

Over the next few weeks, she went out of her way to ask how he was doing with various accounts, and he gave her informal updates on his progress. At one point, he even asked her advice about dealing with one of her more loyal customers who was unhappy with the change of reps. She offered to make a sales call with him to help smooth the customer's anxieties. He accepted. The call went smoothly. Afterward, he bought her lunch and thanked her for her efforts. Away from the group, she found him perfectly acceptable and, at times, even nice. They'd never be close, but it was obvious they could work together.

Her efforts didn't go unnoticed by the rest of the team. Gradually, they started speaking to her more cordially: a simple "how are ya" in the morning without the usual bravado, an occasional sharing of information and, in general, a more relaxed atmosphere at office meetings. Unfortunately, the sales rep's strategy only half worked. In the process of gaining greater acceptance from team members, she lost some momentum. Her numbers never reached the same peak levels again. She can't figure out whether the problem is related to her territory or the fact that she lost her drive to show the guys up.

Office politics are about power and competition. Making them work for you—rather than against you—takes a healthy dose of self-assertion and adaptability. When German philosopher Friedrich Nietzsche said, "Join power with love," he wasn't talking about sleeping your way to the top. He meant using power to do good.

Rather than eschew power (because you associate it with violence), you should seek it out and embrace it. After all, isn't it better for someone like you to have the power to do good? Or would you rather leave it in the hands of all those greedy, unethical people you detest? Just because you dislike the connivers' methods doesn't mean you have to let them win.

Strategy 6: Build Positive Relationships

Positive office politics isn't only about mending fences with workplace enemies. It also involves creating alliances with people who can help you. To increase your feeling of belonging and develop closer relationships within your company, consider taking some of the following steps:

1. Sign up for courses that will improve your communication, team play, and leadership skills. Then try out what you learn on the people who make your life most miserable. Practice until you get it right.
2. Seek out assignments that enable you to work with a variety of colleagues, rather than the same old few you always get stuck with. This will improve your people skills, broaden your visibility, and revitalize your workday. "Even if you're still working in the same company, it can be very energizing to work with new people," says Anderson.
3. Request assignments with people you genuinely like. After hanging out with them a while, you're sure to feel better about yourself and your company.
4. Volunteer for a committee that's working on an interesting issue or project so that you can develop an internal community of colleagues with shared interests and values.
5. When you have the time and energy, pitch in to help others who are on "job overload." You'll build a reputation as a team player and develop a supportive network to help you out should the favor ever need to be returned.
6. Give credit where credit is due. Rather than try to steal the limelight for yourself, share it with others. People will feel better about working for and with you.
7. Be on the lookout for little ways you can foster cooperation instead of conflict. When others sense your attitude, they might mellow, too.
8. Don't harbor grudges. They build ill will and give you ulcers. Chronic anger is a symptom of a serious emotional problem. It has a way of catching up with people who hold onto it too long.

Strategy 7: Stay Positive

Hate is not a productive emotion. It clouds your vision, distorts your judgment, and makes you resent everything and everyone. Hatred kills the spirit and paralyzes you with bitterness. A prominent psychiatrist once commented: "Some of the most self-destructive acts take place in the name of revenge."

Consider, for example, a compensation and benefits manager who was furious with her boss, the senior VP of human resources, for "playing favorites" with another manager. The senior VP vehemently denied this was the case, but she refused to believe him. Instead, she went behind his back—and over his head—to complain about him. Because of the man's outstanding reputation with his superiors, all she managed to do was call attention to the conflict and soil her own standing in the company.

When your emotions are out of control at work, it's always a good idea to take some time to cool down before trying to resolve whatever's bugging you. Accusations made in anger are usually unprofessional, inappropriate, and counterproductive. Once said, they can never be taken back and are seldom forgotten. In the heat of the moment, strong feelings can convert small flare-ups into enduring animosities that can destroy a career.

Rather than go into an emotional tailspin, try (if possible) to develop more of a rational problem-solving approach. For example, the senior VP who'd supposedly been giving preferential treatment realized that the problem was destroying his division's morale. To remedy the situation, he hired a consultant to work with his group to develop better communication and team skills.

Strategy 8: Take Responsibility for Your Own Happiness

If you want to be happier at work, you have to accept responsibility for your own happiness. How? By knowing what you can and can't change. This means evaluating the sources of your dissatisfaction to determine where you can expand your sphere of influence. Often, you can do more than you realize. Because unhappiness (like happiness) is a feeling rather than an objective state of being, you can almost always improve your satisfaction level just by thinking different thoughts. Instead of seeing what's wrong and bad all the time, train your eye to see the positive aspects of a person or situation. Even if the facts never change, you'll feel better.

Knowing what you can change and how to do so is an important key to career satisfaction. On the flip side, it also helps to know what things lie outside your sphere of influence and accept that reality, too.

If you feel lonely at work, make a concerted effort to become more accessible. Develop a list of "social goals" that increase your opportunities for communication and participation. The steps you take should include the following:

1. Volunteer for committees, projects, or task forces that will allow you to work with a variety of people.
2. Ask to serve as a liaison between departments or divisions.
3. Request customer service and/or vendor/supplier relations responsibilities.
4. Make a point of smiling and saying "good morning" to everyone you see on your way in the door.
5. Go out to lunch with your colleagues. Don't eat at your desk.
6. Participate in occasional after-work gatherings.
7. Go to company outings such as annual picnics, golf excursions, and Christmas parties.
8. Carpool to work.
9. Devote time each day to discussing nonwork activities.

10. Don't complain about your workload, job activities, boss, or co-workers. Dwelling on your problems will only make you more unhappy.
11. Praise others' work. You'll make the people you laud and yourself feel good.
12. Make friends with positive people. Avoid perpetual naysayers.
13. Don't participate in mean-spirited gossip.
14. Add the simple phrase, "Thank you," to your everyday vocabulary. A little appreciation can go a long way.

Strategy 9: Don't Confuse Your Job with Your Life

You might not like your job, but it doesn't have to ruin your life. Even if you aren't free to leave, you can always find ways to improve your situation.

Sometimes, the only thing you can really change is your attitude. You might have to work hard, on occasion, to maintain a sense of humor. But have some fun, even if you don't always feel like laughing. By lightening things up, you make your workday more enjoyable. And when the 9-to-5 part of your life goes more smoothly, it tends to make your nightlife better, too.

Every negative has a potential positive:

- If you're bored with your job, you'll have more energy and enthusiasm for the things you do after work, including hobbies, family outings, and community activities.
- If you don't like the people you work with, it'll make you more appreciative of the time you spend with others.
- If office politics are down-and-dirty, what better time to develop some political savvy? You might not like the struggle, but at least you can find something positive in it for you.

Strategy 10: Have a Plan to Get Out

If you hate your job, you should develop a blueprint for leaving, even if you can't implement it immediately. When you know you're actively engaged in creating alternatives, you can put your current situation into a larger context that makes it more tolerable.

"It helps to know that even though you aren't happy now, you won't have to be unhappy forever," says Laurie Anderson. "It's just a question of negotiating the timing."

How to Love the Job You Hate Thought-Starter Worksheet

1. What do you hate most about your job?

   hierarchy that stifles spontaneity; Repetition

2. Do you hate your company's management practices?

   Yes.

3. If so, how would you like to see them changed?

   Each person could have defined tasks that they could complete without going through the boss

4. Is there any way you can influence management policies more?

   No. Maybe

5. Do you hate your boss? If so, why?

Yes & No → means well, appreciates creativity, open to new ideas
paranoid, controlling, oversensitive, insecure, scattered

6. What can you do to improve that relationship?

accept the good with the bad

7. Have you tried to understand your boss's point of view?

Yes

8. If you and your boss are destined not to get along, how much does this affect your peace of mind on a day-to-day basis?

50%

9. Is there another department or division you can transfer to?

no

10. Do you have enough information and contacts throughout the company to transfer into another area?

no,

11. Is your upward mobility stymied?

Not sure

12. Are there any skills, experiences, or horizontal moves you can obtain to get unstuck?

Management?

(continues)

(continued)

13. How do you feel about your co-workers?

Great people

14. Can you honestly say that you've made a concerted effort to get along with the people you work with—even if you don't like them?

Yes

15. Do you consider yourself a competitive person?

A little

16. Does your ambition ever get in the way of cooperation (be honest)?

NO

17. Are you bored with your job responsibilities? If so, can you identify or initiate new activities that'd be more stimulating?

Yes and Yes

18. Is your paycheck the problem?

NO

19. Can you negotiate bonuses or variable-rate increases based on your performance?

X

20. Can you think of any other ways to make your work day and/or environment more satisfying?

Trying

21. If you're committed to staying in a job you dislike, how hard are you really trying to make it better?

a lot, sometimes

22. Have you gotten used to being miserable?

yes and no

23. Can you try harder to be happy?

yes. Stop identifying with my work; develop better hobbies

CHAPTER 7

Layoff Survivors' Dilemma: Put Up or Shut Up

Wherein our hero asks "What in the world am I doing here?"

—Laurence G. Boldt, *Zen and the Art of Making a Living*

When his employer decided to downsize its workforce (yet again), a purchasing agent was given five minutes to say "yea" or "nay" to doubling his workload and keeping his job. With a ton of debts and two small children at home depending on him, he didn't see much of a choice—just one gigantic burden. So instead of walking out the door with the rest of his co-workers, the purchasing agent reluctantly replied "yes." He doesn't feel the least bit grateful for the opportunity to keep his position. On the contrary, he's frustrated, mad, and resentful about being forced to do twice the work for the same amount of money.

The marketing director for a television station feels the same way. She lost half her staff to layoffs, and her workload tripled overnight. Although she doesn't feel she has the luxury to quit, she doesn't have the heart to do the work, either.

It doesn't help that both these professionals also feel they no longer have a voice in what happens in their departments. Such an outlook can wreak havoc on your motivation. A once-energetic and enthusiastic manager can easily become the classic employee who shows up to collect a paycheck but doesn't want to do the work.

Those who do survive "the ax" often feel conflicted. It's called "survivor syndrome." Psychologists often look for it in people who survive disasters such as car or plane wrecks. Now it's afflicting workplace survivors, as well. Although the obvious victims of layoffs are obviously the poor souls who lose their jobs, layoffs can also have a devastating psychological and emotional impact on the surviving employees, too.

"On the one hand you're happy to be alive, a positive emotion," says Columbia Business School professor Joel Brockner, a leading expert on corporate survivor syndrome. "But it's sprinkled in with a heavy dose of negative emotion: 'Maybe it's not over.' 'It could happen to me.'"

Anxiety Rules

Playing musical chairs probably made you anxious when you were a kid. It's 10 times worse now, when the last chair represents a spot on your employer's payroll. Most surviving employees express overwhelmingly negative feelings about the changes that occur in the wake of a downsizing. As Groucho Marx said, "Whatever it is, I'm against it!"

David Noer, vice president of training and education for the Center for Creative Leadership in Greensboro, North Carolina, and author of *Healing the Wounds* (1995, Jossey-Bass), uses a metaphor of surviving children to illustrate the conflicts experienced by employees who remain in a downsized work force.

Imagine a family that's been together for a long time. The loving parents and well-behaved children live in a nurturing, trusting environment. Then, one morning at breakfast, the mother makes an announcement. After reviewing the family budget, she and the father have come to realize that they can't afford to feed and clothe all four of their children. Two of them will have to go. Nothing personal, the father explains. They still love their kids. They just can't afford them anymore.

The next morning at breakfast, two of the chairs have been removed from the table. All evidence of the two missing children is gone. No one says a word about their absence, and any feelings either the parents or the kids have about their absence go unspoken. The parents stress to their remaining children that they should be grateful to be able to stay in the family. To show their appreciation, the children will be expected to take on additional chores that their siblings used to do. The parents assure the kids that this will make them a closer family.

What do you think the children who are left behind are feeling? Sadness at having lost their siblings? Guilt over being allowed to stay in the family? Anger at their parents for changing the rules midstream? Anxiety and panic over their own future? Or perhaps they feel nothing at all because it's too dangerous to feel.

Similarly, survivors of downsized organizations often feel depressed, paranoid, angry, numb, and betrayed. Couple that with reduced commitment, risk-taking, and spontaneity and you have the formula for what Noer terms, "Layoff Survivor Sickness"—a paralyzing condition caused by the profound shift in the psychological employment contract between individuals and organizations.

You can point the finger of blame at your employer, but it won't help much. Most layoffs are an inevitable consequence of new social and economic forces, not organizational malice and incompetence. And although many organizations bungle the layoff process badly, you must accept the responsibility for managing your own career amid the chaos if you choose to stay with the company.

Get in Touch with Your Emotions

"After a downsizing, the environment can be like emotional quicksand," says Englewood, Colorado, career counselor Linda Bougie. "There's a real loss of control, like everything that's happening is out of your hands."

Maureen Gold, the director of Baxter Healthcare Corporation's career center in Deerfield, Illinois, agrees: "When an organization is going through a lot of change, it's harder for people to take control of their careers because the overwhelming message is that you don't have control."

Your first goal should be to take stock of your feelings and, if necessary, make some positive deposits into your emotional bank account. How can you do this? Synergies are hard to achieve when your company is downsizing. Knowing that, your goal is to rebuild damaged relationships and forge new alliances with people in the organization you still esteem and trust. Says Gold: "People you respect can be energy sources that keep you motivated."

Although you might feel compelled to avoid mentioning the layoffs when talking with colleagues, emotional honesty can go a long way in an anxiety-ridden environment. On the other hand, unexpressed fears and feelings tend to gain power and momentum, sabotaging relationships and paralyzing productivity.

If you're a manager, you can help interrupt that cycle, and it won't cost the company a thing. Simply encourage your people to express their feelings and fears openly. But don't react negatively to what they say. Also, let them know that what they're experiencing is perfectly natural under the circumstances. Talking about your own feelings can establish a healthy atmosphere for discussion. One senior manager was able to reconnect effectively with his staff this way. "Believe me," he told them sincerely, "I feel as bad about this as you do."

Similarly, an operations manager called a meeting in which all of his remaining group members were encouraged to vent feelings and discuss personal reactions to the layoffs. Noer says such "leading from the heart" is critical to the recovery and success of downsized organizations.

If you aren't an executive, you can still improve your situation by encouraging your boss to open up the lines of feelings and communication. Rather than wait like a powerless child to see what your crazy company is going to foist on you next, why not find your own voice and message amidst the confusion?

Think about those metaphorical children. What if they stood up to their parents and said: "Your priorities don't make any sense to us. Isn't there a way to improve our finances without destroying our family?" What if they suggested more acceptable alternatives to breaking up the home? For example, the kids could work after school to supplement the family income through paper routes, dog walking, or lemonade stands. They could volunteer to live with a treasured aunt and uncle until finances got better. Or, perhaps the family could cut expenses by renting out rooms or moving into a smaller place.

Devise New Solutions

There are always other options. Maybe you can help your employer discover better solutions. That's what happened at Rhino Foods Inc., a dessert manufacturer in Burlington, Vermont. At a companywide meeting, management announced that business had slowed so much that they could no longer justify the number of people on staff. Then they invited employees to find a way to solve the problem, and 26 jumped at the chance.

After studying the issues for three weeks, the group developed the idea of an Employee Exchange Program, an in-house temporary-employment agency that "lends" extra workers to other companies. Employees who volunteer for assignments are interviewed, hired, and paid by the "host" company, but they retain their benefits through Rhino. And if the host company has a lower hourly wage, Rhino makes up the difference. So far, the only downside has been more paperwork. But then layoffs create additional paperwork, too.

Manage Others' Expectations of You

It can be hard not to act out, to remember that you're an adult and a professional who was hired because your employer believed you had the skills and desire to help the organization achieve its goals. So many adults regress and start acting like children who have no place to go and no one to play with.

An investment banker who works for a New York–based firm managed to "stay adult" and professional despite institutional obstacles. When the banker was asked to join his firm's restructuring task force, he knew it would be important to participate. He also knew that the responsibility would be like having a second full-time job. His dilemma: how to handle both duties without working 18- or 20-hour days. What he needed, he decided, was to work smarter but not necessarily harder.

His three rules of participation were the following:

1. **Never work more than a 12-hour day.** A devoted family man, he acknowledged openly that spending evenings at home with his wife and two daughters was important for his sanity. Although he was willing to begin his workday early (6 a.m.), he also planned to be on the 6:15 p.m. train home. You could set your watch by him. Unless it was an absolute emergency, he never deviated from his schedule. As a result, his employers and co-workers knew exactly what to expect from him.
2. **Don't expect perfection.** By nature, he was a meticulous man who dotted every *i* and crossed every *t*. He also knew that if he maintained that work style, he'd soon fall far behind. So he lost the perfectionist mentality and developed personal standards of "good enough" that kept his reputation for able work intact.
3. **Share your goals.** Always considered a star performer, the banker knew he could never produce the same results with so much added responsibility. Rather than try to achieve some impossible goal, he renegotiated his sales objectives with his manager and then worked diligently to deliver what he'd promised. Not once did he beat himself up for not delivering the sales figures he'd achieved in previous years. However, getting his manager to buy into his new goals was crucial to his success. Otherwise, it would merely have looked as if his performance was way off.

Unlike other highly motivated and ambitious professionals, this savvy careerist didn't get seduced into taking on more than he could possibly accomplish. By managing the expectations of the people around him, he preserved his own energy and enthusiasm for his work.

Accept Your Limitations

While acknowledging that you're neither a machine nor a superhuman always carries some risk, you don't do anyone a favor by refusing to accept or understand your personal and professional limitations. "Unless you learn to set boundaries and prioritize your work, you can end up going down with the ship," says Bougie. That's exactly what happened to the assistant dean of a prestigious liberal-arts college in Chicago. When his support staff was eliminated, the administrator didn't adjust his goals to accommodate that loss. Instead, he tried valiantly to do the job of three people. In his case, this meant single-handedly servicing more than 1,200 students. His reward: ulcerated colitis. He also got a year off, which he needed to recover his health and sanity.

An operations analyst with a consulting group in Chicago had better success with a more aggressive style. To prevent an overload of demand on her energies, she moved her office to a location removed from her colleagues. She also convinced her manager to let her work at home two mornings a week in order to get some uninterrupted work time.

Keep in mind, though, that even your most innovative solutions won't be considered seriously unless you have a solid track record of professional credibility. You need to establish yourself as a hardworking and committed team player who's willing to go the extra mile before asking your employer to go out of the way for you.

Make a Commitment to Be Part of the Solution

When an assistant marketing manager attended a friend's wedding instead of the company's largest promotional event in history, his priority for friendship wasn't much appreciated. Although no ultimatum was given, he had trouble recovering from the perception that he wasn't committed to organizational goals and priorities.

Balancing work and personal needs is a tricky business in organizations where the work seems to mushroom out of control. To get what you want for yourself, you must demonstrate a genuine commitment to the company's efforts as well.

People who get ahead in downsizing organizations are the ones who take the initiative to be part of the solution rather than the problem. Instead of railing against the boss, they do their best to add value wherever they can.

When Baxter Healthcare Corporation began its downsizing initiatives 10 years ago, it needed a human resources professional to staff its outplacement center. No one wanted the job because it seemed too temporary. Now, 10 years later, many people who thought that job would be too short-lived are gone and Maureen Gold (who accepted it) is still there going strong. In fact, the company's career center has not only outlived its skeptics, it's become one of the more enduring parts of the organization. In the process, Maureen Gold has discovered her own professional mission. A former teacher, she loves "to see the light bulb go on in people's heads when they realize they have choices."

Gold's message is one of empowerment. Regardless of whether you stay with the company or leave, she says, the important thing is to realize that it's still up to you to manage your career. "Through all the craziness, you can find opportunities to grow," she says.

Attitude Is a Key Variable

When a national chain of bookstores consolidated its operations and eliminated several suburban stores, the company's advertising manager suddenly found herself saddled with public relations responsibilities as well. Although she hadn't been familiar with PR, she viewed it as a "learning opportunity"—a chance to expand her skills and experience into other arenas.

"I could have sat around moaning that I'm not a PR person, or that PR isn't my job," she says today. "But what good would it have done? Like it or not, I'm a PR person now. Fortunately, it's kind of fun."

To maintain your sanity and self-esteem, you need to accept responsibility for your decision to stay. If you can't do that, make arrangements to leave. After all, what's the point of holding onto your job if you end up becoming a physically and emotionally charred wreck in the process?

"When you accept that you're 100 percent responsible for who you are and where you work, you lose the need to blame others or hold them emotionally hostage," says Linda Bougie.

After that, there can be a joy in staying, says Gold. When you're able to see the changes around you as an opportunity to invest in yourself, you won't feel like you're just holding onto your job. You'll realize that you're developing skills and experience you can take with you when you leave. "In this day and age, everybody needs to learn how be a change manager," says Gold. "It's the most marketable skill there is." Unfortunately, most employees are so busy bemoaning their fates that they lose out on that window of opportunity.

"Survivors are afraid to get their hopes up," says Phyllis Edelen, a human resources consultant in Dallas, Texas, who's managed career centers for AT&T and Kraft Foods. "Instead of getting involved, they sit around waiting for the other shoe to fall." She understands their fears but questions their lack of motivation. "People may be waiting for the next disaster, but in the meantime, they don't do anything to prepare themselves for that day," says Edelen. "Despite all that mental anguish they put themselves through, it hits them just as hard when they do get laid off."

No job lasts forever, so why waste the time you have worrying about when the boom will strike? If you've chosen to stay (at least for now), focus instead on self-development. Use the days, weeks, and months ahead to build some new skills (including job search skills), experiences, and contacts that will enable you to build bridges out of your current situation.

View This as a Learning Opportunity

Yolanda Banks is a survivor who rose to that particular challenge. Banks is an environmental coordinator for a medical manufacturing plant in Niles, Illinois, that had a two-year plan to close down its local operation and relocate elsewhere. Every round of layoffs brought her one round closer to the day when she, too, must go. It also meant saying goodbye to treasured friends and co-workers, many of whom considered themselves fortunate to be among the first to leave.

For those who remained behind, a bitter legacy awaited them. For years, they'd worked together to make the plant a productive facility—and they'd succeeded. Now, everything they worked so hard to build had to be systematically dismantled.

Animosities ran rampant. Many people were frustrated and bitter. Productivity plummeted along with morale. The potential for accidents skyrocketed every day. Ordinarily, this would not be Banks's problem. But her manager didn't survive the first round of cuts and she did, which made her the ad hoc manager of safety and environmental health. She didn't have the title and she certainly didn't get a pay raise, but she accepted the responsibility. To do her job well meant to ensure the safety and good health of her co-workers. For her, that was more important than any personal grudges she harbored against her employer for closing its doors or doubling her workload.

Banks's attitude made her different. In an environment riddled with fear, mistrust, and anger, motivation was low and risk-taking almost nonexistent. Almost all the employees were nursing their wounds and waiting to leave. It had become bad form to show any enthusiasm or excitement for your job, let alone your employer, who was, in everyone's eyes, Public Enemy Number One. Still, Banks understood that you can't discover and express your talents while hiding under a rock and hoping the winds of change will blow over.

Even in an organization that's redefining itself, there are things to be learned and accomplished on your way out the door. As Maureen Gold says, "It makes a difference how you leave."

Yolanda Banks had never been a manager before, so this was her big chance to become one. She admitted she could use a mentor. But there wasn't one available. She had to learn to mentor herself. Fortunately, she had the mental skill to do it.

To self-mentor, you have to be your own best role model. Create the prototype and then live it. This means taking responsibility for learning what you need to know to do your job. Banks is a good teacher who knows how to ask the right questions. This quality will allow her to resolve the problems she faces. When a drum of questionable origin showed up on the dock, for example, she used her research and investigative skills to figure out where it came from and how to dispose of it.

Banks already knew an important principle of leadership: Don't wait for someone else to solve a problem. Instead, take the initiative to solve it yourself. That same initiative appeared again when the plant manager was seeking ways to motivate his remaining personnel to meet productivity standards and goals.

Toward that end, Banks recommended (and piloted) a stress ergonomics program that, for very little money, was already being implemented successfully at companies such as 3M. Stress ergonomics is a fancy name for a simple 10-minute stretch break, which (as most fitness experts will tell you) can do wonders to boost energy levels. The program has 98 percent participation, but it doesn't play entirely to rave reviews. In spite of many enthusiastic supporters, it also has its fair share of detractors. Some say it's a ridiculous waste of time. Others agree it's a nice program—but too short and way too late (they complain the company should have instituted the plan years ago).

Don't Let Others Hold You Back

When you approach your job with creativity and enthusiasm, don't expect the people around you to rave, "Wow! What a great person!" More likely than not, you'll encounter what Hawaiians refer to as a "crabpot mentality."

When Hawaiian fishermen go crabbing, they throw the crabs they catch into a bucket with no lid. The Hawaiians learned long ago that there was no danger of the crabs climbing out and scurrying away. Whenever one crab reaches the lip of the bucket, the leader is pulled back into the pot by the others, who seem determined not to let any members of their group escape. Who needs a jail warden when you have each other to guard the gates?

Granted, great ideas are hard to achieve in downsizing organizations where emotional leakage and miscommunication run high. But that doesn't mean you shouldn't try. Why not lose the chip on your shoulder and show some initiative of your own? For those of you with leadership blood in your veins, the time is ripe to separate yourself from the horde of naysayers that surrounds you. Exercise your leadership potential and you'll truly stand out.

Managers (and aspiring managers) should display the courage to participate in the changes and, if possible, make change a more compassionate experience. Norbert Wiener, the founder of Cybernetics, said, "The world may be viewed as a myriad of 'to-whom-it-may-concern messages.'" It's up to you whether you want to heed their call. If you do, expect the road to get rocky.

A senior customer service manager who'd made it through two years of continuous organizational change (including five different restructuring attempts) was determined to be more than just a survivor. He wanted to learn something from the process, even if it meant putting his personal career objectives on hold for a while. To him, it was a "developmental challenge" to keep his staff motivated and provide quality customer service in a constantly changing environment.

His advice: Use organizational change to become an expert in what you do. For example, he was able to experiment with a dozen different ways to improve customer service, even in the midst of business and staff changes. The hardest part was to keep his staff of 60 people motivated to provide quality service in the face of serious morale problems. Secrecy, he discovered, was his enemy. Communication—even if it meant over-communication—was his greatest ally. By sharing his concerns and frustrations with the staff, he motivated them to work hard, even if the company they worked for didn't seem to appreciate their efforts.

"I wore a lot of hats with my staff," says the manager. "Protector, advisor, parent. Sometimes, they acted like little kids who needed a 'time out' to get control of themselves. It was tough."

Getting through the rough times might be easier if you recognize that you've entered a skill-building phase in your career that will make you more marketable elsewhere. "If I hadn't known that my situation would be temporary," says the customer service manager, "I probably would've been miserable."

As it is, he isn't sorry that his name showed up on a list of jobs to be cut. "Mentally, I'd already packed my bags," he says. "The paperwork was just a formality." Now that he's in the job market again, he's discovering that many employers are interested in his ability to manage through change. This is fine with him, but he has a requirement of his own: He wants to manage change that comes from growth rather than shrinkage. "I want to add staff and grow them," he says. "Not fire people I've groomed as members of my team." To achieve that goal, he's targeting expanding midsize companies with solid market niches.

Be Prepared to Walk Away

Sometimes, breaking the ties of organizational dependency means walking away from a place where you no longer want to work. When a Midwest hospital reorganized its social-work department and moved it under the rubric of nursing, the director didn't appreciate his resulting demotion and return to a direct-service role. The director couldn't afford to quit outright, but he decided to work on developing an effective search strategy that would enable him to find something else quickly. If that didn't work out, he planned to develop a private counseling practice. If he was going to do direct service, he wanted to get paid real money for it!

Remember the purchasing agent discussed earlier in this chapter—the one who had only five minutes to decide his fate? His experience taught him an important lesson: Be ready for anything. From that day on, he worked diligently to pay his bills and prepare himself financially to walk away. During the next reorganization, he got his chance. When two more positions were eliminated from his department, he again had five minutes to decide whether he wanted to triple his workload in order to stay. He didn't need five minutes to decide. He was out of there in two. "I expected them to ask me to pick up the trash and throw out the garbage, too," he says bitterly. "It was a setup to fail. No one can do the job of six people."

He doesn't regret the decision. Indeed, he looks forward to seeking out new challenges. "I want the challenge of growth and opportunity," he says. "I have no desire to be some overworked workhorse."

Knowing how and when to get out of an abusive employment situation is an important vocational skill. Although you shouldn't ever plant your flag around issues and concerns that don't really bother you, you do need the gumption to say when necessary, "I refuse to let life (or my employer) do this to me."

If you can't make peace with the new terms of your employment, you must find a way to walk away. Whatever you do, don't be a victim. There's no pleasure in the role and no opportunity for the future. Stand up and be counted instead. You'll be better off for having made the effort.

Even if they're relieved to still have a job, layoff survivors experience mostly downbeat emotions about their work situations. In *Healing the Wounds* (1995, Jossey-Bass), author David Noer describes the following survivor fears and concerns:

- **Job insecurity.** This effect cuts across all levels: People go home at night wondering whether they'll still have a job tomorrow, next week, or next month.
- **Lack of management credibility.** After a downsizing, management becomes the ubiquitous "they." Even executives blame higher-ups for their problems and try to separate themselves from them. Apparently, there's still some gratification in being a victim, not the oppressor. Also, employees often feel that the wrong people got "kept," while the "good guys" got kicked out.
- **Depression, stress, and fatigue.** Such symptoms are common at all levels of the organization. Battle fatigue is bound to set in when you must do more work with less resources at a time when your motivation is at an all-time low.
- **Distrust and betrayal.** These are everywhere. A "watch-your-back" attitude becomes prevalent, creating a hostile, alienated workforce and workplace.
- **Lack of reciprocal commitment.** Some employees maintain loyalty to their employer; however, no one believes the company will do the same.
- **Wanting it to be over.** Workforce reductions are draining and stressful. You might feel like you're hanging on by a thread waiting for it all to end.

- **Poor planning and communication.** In a workplace that's likely characterized by secrecy, mistrust, and power struggles, employees thirst for direct communication, more information, and some little sign that a benign authority is in charge somewhere.
- **Short-term thinking.** Management usually gets labeled as greedy—fixated on short-term profits. This perception is sometimes true, but not always. Some companies try to balance concern for next quarter's profits with long-term goals.
- **Permanent instability.** Employees feel that change—and not necessarily for the better—will be a constant at the company forevermore.
- **Long-lasting wounds.** The Noer research shows that even five years after a downsizing, the survivor syndrome lingers on in the form of fatigue, decreased motivation, sadness, depression, insecurity, anxiety, fear, and anger. Add to that a sense of resignation and psychic numbing and you have a prescription for a demoralized workforce desperately in need of emotional repair.

Layoff Survivors' Dilemma Thought-Starter Worksheet

1. Have you ever survived a corporate restructuring? (If you answered "no," please skip to question 11.)

____

2. What's the toughest organizational challenge your current employer is facing?

____

____

____

3. How would you advise your employer to handle that problem?

4. What happened to your job when your organization downsized?

5. Are you satisfied with your new role?

6. Do you have enough time and resources to do your new job? If not, is there any way you can gain greater control over the situation?

7. Do you have a new boss as a result of the downsizing?

8. If you have a new boss, do you feel that your boss is someone you can work with? If not, why?

(continues)

(continued)

9. If you don't get along with your new boss, is there anything you can do to improve that relationship?

____

____

____

10. Can you transfer to a different department or division?

____

11. If you've never been through a downsizing, what do you imagine it will be like? What do you think will happen to your job?

____

____

____

12. Do you know anyone who survived a downsizing? Is there anything you can learn from that person's experience?

____

____

____

13. Do you think your company might go through a downsizing in the future?

____

14. If you answered "yes" to question 13, what are you doing to prepare yourself for that day?

____

____

____

15. If you answered "nothing" to question 14, is there anything you can do to prepare yourself now (for example, start networking within the organization, write your resume, join a professional group)?

____

____

____

16. Who do you share your anxieties and concerns with? Are these people helpful?

____

____

17. If your support system isn't helpful, have you considered professional assistance?

____

CHAPTER 8

Quitting Your Job

Leave them while you're looking good.

—Anita Loos

When the great Impressionist painter Paul Gauguin ditched his boring job as a stockbroker and skipped off to Tahiti, he lived out an escapist fantasy that most people would confine to their daydreams or weekend getaways. Depending on your perspective, you might consider Gauguin courageous (for living out his desires) or immature (for abandoning his obligations). Mrs. Gauguin was probably not too thrilled with his decision, whereas art lovers everywhere are likely to applaud his bravado.

The magnitude of his accomplishments might color your vision. If you knew you had the talent of a Gauguin, you might run off to a tropical paradise to paint, too. Possessing more ordinary skills might make you think twice.

But did Gauguin really possess some fabulous innate artistic genius or, more likely, an incredible drive to bring his talents to fruition? By taking the initiative to explore his dream, he discovered a wellspring of potential within himself. Who knows what might happen to you if you could devote your full attention to developing your potential? However you judge Gauguin—as a great artist, as an immature guy in the throes of a midlife crisis, or both—it's clear his tremendous talent would never have seen the light of day if he hadn't also had the ability to throw convention to the winds and live as he pleased.

Of course, his approach wouldn't work for everybody. The point is that he found a unique solution, which led to a uniquely satisfying accomplishment and lifestyle.

You might very well place your family responsibilities and financial obligations above your duty to fulfill your personal potential. This, too, is a valid choice. What you need to question, however, is whether you're being unnecessarily shortsighted. If you see yourself as someone without a lot of talent or potential to fulfill, it's easy to idealize your loyalties and stay right where you are.

There are many good reasons not to make changes. Lack of self-confidence isn't one of them, especially if you're really unhappy with your current job or career. Even if you never aspire to great achievements, you can aspire to happiness. But don't expect it to fall in your lap. You have to go out and find it.

Believing that you could never have a truly satisfying career is just a way of justifying inertia, says career counselor Mike Murphy with the Signet Group in Chicago, Illinois. "When all the choices you make are based on a false premise, the conclusions that flow from that premise are likely to be false, too," says Murphy. "How can you know there's nothing out there for you when you haven't even looked?" Too often, says Murphy, "we convince ourselves we *can't* do what really we're *afraid* to do."

Gauguin might have gone to extremes, but most people dream too small, making unnecessary sacrifices in the name of some misunderstood "reality."

The Lies We Tell Ourselves

Before you conclude that you have no choice but to stay in a job or occupation that isn't right for you, take some time to examine your beliefs. Leave open the possibility that some assumptions you've been making about yourself might be more self-fulfilling prophecy than objective reality.

In *Divorcing a Corporation* (1986, Random House), Jacqueline Horor Plumez identified a host of self-defeating lies that many of us use to talk ourselves into staying put when we should be letting go. "This way of thinking comes with a very dear price tag: You. Your aspirations. Your needs. Your happiness," says Plumez.

To break free of that psychological bondage, you need to recognize these self-deceptions for what they are—a way to prevent yourself from getting hurt by not trying. The following sections discuss some of the "lies that bind."

Lie 1: It Would Be Disloyal of Me to Look Around

A 20-year veteran of the Bell system swelled with pride when describing himself as a "loyal corporate foot soldier." By that, he meant his employer could count on him to go wherever and do whatever he was asked. If his career path looked more like a potpourri of jobs than a logical progression of upward moves, he took comfort in knowing that he was needed. In exchange for that sacrifice, he expected them to find a place for him for as long as he wanted to work.

Divestiture didn't sit well with him, but he never dreamed it would affect him directly. When his name showed up on a list of people classified as "available for reassignment," he assumed he'd be picked up by another division immediately. Even after receiving his 60-day notice, he refused to look outside the company.

Only after he was actually forced off the payroll did the foolishness of his ways occur to him. Loyalty was supposed to be a two-way street, but he was the only one honoring the contract. When the company no longer needed him, he was discarded like yesterday's newspaper, without a second thought for his welfare. It was a hard lesson, and he was ill-prepared to handle the emotional fallout. Had he recognized sooner that the changes in company structure signaled the end of their psychological employment contract, he could have taken more steps to protect himself. But by closing his eyes too long to reality, he ended up frightened and cynical—scrambling for his livelihood in a competitive workplace he couldn't begin to understand.

When you tell yourself you can't betray your company's loyalty by leaving, you abdicate responsibility for your own future and, some would say, betray yourself instead. Trust me: If a company really needs you, it'll make every attempt to keep you should you decide to leave.

For example, a technical trainer who gave the traditional two weeks' notice was offered a consulting contract to complete the projects she still had pending. In another case, a hospital that didn't want to lose one of its most productive administrators made an exceptional counteroffer to entice him to stay. Neither of these professionals confused their new agreements with loyalty oaths. But, for both, it was a recognition that the work they did was valued enough to motivate their employers to keep them on the payroll a while longer.

Lie 2: I Might Fail Somewhere Else

By the time she finally made the decision to quit, the technical trainer who'd been offered a consulting contract to stay had convinced herself that no employer would ever want to hire her. To her amazement, she was off the payroll less than one week when a former vendor extended her a job offer. This isn't the only time I've seen perfectly capable professionals talk themselves into believing they're worthless and incompetent. Low self-esteem and interpersonal conflicts with bosses or co-workers are often at the heart of this self-defeating scenario.

A little reality testing can go a long way toward checking such self-destructive fantasies (and they usually are fantasies). By networking with people who'd worked with her before, the technical trainer got some objective feedback on her performance that helped mitigate her anxieties.

If a lack of self-confidence is blocking your ability to seek out better opportunities, it might help to test the job market before reaching any final decisions. You can make a commitment to look around without making a commitment to leave. Should your first foray into the job market reveal that you are, in fact, missing a crucial skill or piece of experience, you can establish short-term goals for yourself that will fill that gap. Then, when you've built the necessary expertise, you'll be able to move on.

Should you discover (as many do) that no one has a lower opinion of you than yourself, you might want to consider professional counseling. A major self-esteem problem can really get in the way of your success.

Lie 3: I'll Never Make as Much Money Anywhere Else

Having worked your way up to a respectable salary level, it's understandable that you'd resist giving up one cent of those hard-earned dollars. Before you turn this self-defeating lie into a showstopper, though, you might want to examine your assumptions more closely. Odds are, you haven't investigated the job market thoroughly enough to know whether you'd earn less elsewhere. You might just be using money as an excuse to keep you from testing the waters. Again, you can make a commitment to look without making a commitment to leave. At least that way, you can base your decisions on logic and fact rather than folklore.

Before the technical trainer left her large corporate employer for a smaller consulting firm, she, too, assumed that she'd have to take a significant hit on the money. In fact, the firm's offer did come in $5,000 short. She was so sure she'd have to take a pay cut, she didn't think about negotiating for more. After some coaching, though, she was able to convince her new employer to meet her salary needs. What's more, she was told they would have been disappointed in her if she hadn't counter-offered. So much for her assumptions!

As a professional, your first goal should be to build the most impressive skill set possible so that you can command more money in the marketplace. Your second task is to research and target companies that can really capitalize on the things you have to offer.

During interviews, you must do your utmost to convince hiring managers of the value you bring with you. After you show you can solve their organizational problems, you can explain how much it will cost them. Then, come back and tell me no employer will match your current salary and (maybe) I'll believe you.

Lie 4: Maybe Things Will Get Better

If you wait them out, some work situations do improve. But the outcome depends on how or why they got worse in the first place. Nine years ago, a human resources generalist joined a major health-care corporation. Six months later, she was involved in her first reorganization. Although she survived with her job intact, her workload virtually doubled overnight.

"Don't worry," her manager told her. "Things will get better." That was more than eight years ago. Since then, she's been through five different restructurings. Whenever she wasn't personally affected, she was laying others off.

She just can't get excited about these changes anymore. She's heard lies too many times. Still, she's reluctant to leave. She has nine years in—long enough to know her way around the system and feel comfortable with lots of people. Besides, she's still convinced she can find a safe part of the company that won't be restructured. Some people have trouble learning from experience, I guess.

Lie 5: It's My Fault I'm Not Happy

Blaming yourself for not liking your job won't solve any problems. If you want to take more responsibility for your happiness, you need to think in terms of "mismatch," not faultfinding. Trying to understand why your job, company, or field doesn't suit your needs will help you redirect your energies toward creating a better match.

For example, a social worker found the family counseling center she worked at too much like a dysfunctional family, with everyone over-involved in everyone else's business. Whereas most of her co-workers loved the "family feeling" of the place, she felt guilty for wanting an atmosphere that encouraged more professionalism and greater independence. Eventually, she came to realize that leaving the agency was like growing up and leaving home. At a certain time in life, it's definitely the right thing to do. Once she figured that out, she knew it would be crazy to stay.

You can come up with a million (untrue) reasons why you can't leave a situation you dislike. But when you deny reality (or the depth of your unhappiness), it has a way of catching up with you. If you do nothing to remedy the situation you hate, there's a good chance you'll end up being terminated. You might try to hide your feelings from co-workers, but negativity has a way of seeping out when you least expect it. Most of us don't have very good poker faces.

This is exactly what happened to a sales rep with an aluminum-siding company who wanted to work in a more glamorous industry. While he vacillated about whether to stay or to go, he stopped paying enough attention to his numbers. They dipped way below quota, and before he realized what was happening, he had three months of severance pay and carte blanche to find something that suited him better.

Likewise, an office manager was so bored with performing the same old duties day in and day out that she could barely manage to drag herself to the office in the morning, and never before 9:30. From there, it was a short step to long lunch hours and even longer weekends. Only a Neanderthal could have missed her lack of motivation. Like the sales rep, she got her walking papers along with three months' pay to figure out what she wanted to do next.

Timing Your Departure

You might wonder: Is it better to look for a job while you still have one, or to quit first so that you can take the time to look for something better? It depends.

Both the sales rep and the office manager were relieved to be set free from positions that weren't right for them. Although it's never smart to get yourself thrown out because you lacked the courage to leave on your own accord, there is an argument for taking the time to search out what you really want. But if you don't have enough of a financial cushion, panic over money might force you into a premature decision.

Also, being unemployed can make you more insecure during interviews, especially if you fear an employer might try to take advantage of you as a result. However, no one can take advantage of you unless you let them. Having confidence in your own abilities and worth is the best antidote against that happening.

Cultivating Good References

If you burn bridges on your way out the door, you complicate your situation with poor references. This could make you pretty defensive in interviews, and you'll have to supply more positive references. If necessary, you'll have to let your former employers know that it's against the law for them to say anything that would interfere with your ability to find a new job. Know your rights here and, if necessary, exercise them.

Unemployed professionals aren't the only ones with sticky reference problems. Unless your bosses know you're looking for a new job, you won't be able to use their names as references. Plus, it's hard to activate the kind of network you need for an effective search if you must keep your job hunt secret. You might have to avoid a huge chunk of opportunities because you're afraid to reveal your search to key people who would otherwise be able to help you.

Besides quitting outright, you have two choices: You can discreetly tell certain trusted networking contacts that you're in the market and ask them to please honor your confidence. Your second option is to tell your employer that you're looking. Although risky, this strategy has worked surprisingly well for some people. Although some employers become furious at being abandoned, others have been known to respond more maturely.

Anyway, when it comes to changing jobs, there's always risk. It's up to you to choose which risks you prefer.

Job Hunting While You're Still Employed

If you can start job hunting discreetly while still employed, you'll have more time to do the preparatory work it takes to research the job market, write a resume, and probe your network. However, after you've gauged the market (and your marketability), you might want to risk leaving your job without having another. Why? Looking for a job is a full-time job. To find a position in a company that's really right for you takes time, energy, and commitment. That's not something you have in great reserve when you're still physically and emotionally committed to another position.

A retail store manager promised herself for more than a year that she'd look for a new position. But beyond responding to want ads, she was simply too tired at the end of the day to do the kind of networking she needed to be successful. Because she hoped to change careers into media sales, she needed extra time and energy for the task. She couldn't seem to mobilize herself to do more than the bare minimum, though.

Finally, she made a commitment to leave. Her plan included an interim job as a department store salesperson to keep some money coming in. Knowing she could meet her basic financial needs relieved a great burden. When she was able to job hunt in earnest, she was incredibly aggressive in pursuing leads and successfully found a new position within two months.

An Emotional Journey

The process of letting go of a job that's holding you back usually sets an important emotional process in motion. Even if you're more than ready to leave, expect a bit of an emotional roller coaster on your way out the door.

For the technical trainer discussed earlier in this chapter, resolving anger at her boss and co-workers for not respecting her work and for mistreating her was the primary emotional task. At times, her anger was fueled by anxiety that she wouldn't be able to find another position; at other times, it was tempered by her success in the outside world. When she saw she'd be able to find something else rather easily, her rage melted away—a sure sign that her hostile dependency on them had vanished. The offer of consulting work was the ultimate coup de grace. Finally, they recognized and appreciated her competence, paving the way for her to exit the once-stormy relationship gracefully. Leaving properly is an emotional challenge.

No matter how much you dislike the work, you can still feel a twinge of regret when you're training your successor. No one likes being a lame duck. It's no fun to be left out of the action. Yet letting go piece-by-piece can be an important part of leaving.

Missing Your Friends and Routine

There's almost always someone you're going to miss. And although you promise each other you'll stay in touch, even friendships that extend beyond the office corridors can lose momentum without daily contact or shared experiences. You might also find yourself grieving the loss of your comfortable, familiar routine.

You'll get over it. When you find a new position, you'll make new friends and establish new routines. But if you quit without having anyplace new to go, you might find yourself feeling empty, disoriented, and unsure of who you are or where you're going. This "neutral zone" is an in-between state where you've left one place behind but don't yet know what lies ahead. You must pass through this important transition point before you can see clearly where you're headed. If you jump from one job to another without allowing time to separate emotionally, you might have trouble reconnecting. Then you might carry all your old emotional baggage (in the form of unresolved conflicts) into your new job and end up repeating the cycle of dissatisfaction.

Do Your Homework to Find the Right Situation

It hardly seems worth the effort of leaving just to be unhappy somewhere else. The only way to prevent that from happening is to make sure that you understand the true sources of your dissatisfaction so that you don't seek out places or situations where those conditions are likely to recur. This means sorting through whether it was the job, the company, or the people you worked with that created the mismatch for you. When you know, you can ask the right questions and evaluate jobs more clearly to make sure that your history doesn't repeat itself.

Before you ever job-hunt, you really need to understand what you like to do, what you do best, and the kind of places where you like to work. Then you must have the courage and persistence to seek opportunities that can really meet your needs.

Saying Farewell

After you find a great new job, your next challenge will be to find a way to break the news to your employer. Perhaps you prefer the Johnny Paycheck method: You know, the one where you shout, "You can take this job and shove it" over your shoulder as you storm out the door.

Steps for Leaving Your Job Gracefully

1. Decide how much notice you would like to give. Two weeks is standard. For high-level professional and executive positions, allow slightly longer if possible.
2. Schedule a face-to-face meeting with your boss to express simply your intention to leave, the date of departure, and appreciation for the opportunity to work with the company. Make sure that your boss is the first person in the company who knows of your intention and that the work has not spread to the office grapevine ahead of you.
3. Try to negotiate the terms of your leave-taking fairly. Review your projects to determine an orderly transfer of responsibilities. If possible, finish those projects that you can realistically finish in the allotted time.
4. Offer to train your replacement. If no successor has been chosen by your last day, volunteer to make yourself available by telephone for a week or two after you've left.
5. Prepare your written resignation after your resignation meeting. Address it to your boss, with a carbon copy to the human resources department. Confirm your intention to leave and your last day of employment. Don't elaborate on your reasons. Keep the memo short and upbeat because it will remain in your permanent employment record long after you're gone.
6. Schedule an exit meeting with human resources to assess your benefits. Review your insurance benefits. Determine your last day of health coverage. If you're entitled to pension or profit-sharing money, make sure you know exactly how much you should receive and when you'll be paid. Be sure to fill out all necessary forms.
7. Beware of counteroffers. If you're tempted by one, review the reasons you decided to leave. If they're still valid, proceed with your plan of action and politely decline.

8. Handle yourself professionally and responsibly at all times. Resignations can cause hard feelings. Never burn bridges. You never know when you'll need to be in contact with those people and this organization again.

Anger not your forte? Maybe you'd rather procrastinate for weeks, practicing your resignation speech in front of the mirror as if you were receiving an Academy Award for Best Actor. Then, on the day of the blessed event, you rush into the personnel office and blurt "I quit" into the astonished secretary's face.

If you're a really timid type who'll do anything to avoid a confrontation, you might want to wait until late Friday night when no one else is around, slip your resignation letter under the boss's office door, and then sneak out the back like the Benedict Arnold you are.

Or maybe you're the silent type who leaves at 5 p.m. with everyone else, cheerfully waving goodbye to your co-workers. Little do they know you aren't coming back—ever. On Monday morning, your phone is disconnected (just in case they try to call) and your mail carrier has instructions to stamp letters from the company, "addressee unknown." Running away like this has its downside: You can never answer your telephone or doorbell again.

There might be 50 ways to leave your lover, but there's only one good way to leave your job: Give ample notice of your intentions, express your appreciation for the experience, make arrangements for an orderly transition, and say goodbye—nicely.

Leave like a grown-up and a professional, and your old employer just might treat you that way.

Quitting Your Job Thought-Starter Worksheet

1. Have you ever quit a job? Or left a relationship?

2. How did it make you feel to say goodbye? Were you sad? Guilt-ridden? Angry? Relieved?

3. How long did it take you to make the decision to leave?

4. Was there a "straw that broke the camel's back"? If so, what was it?

5. Are you sorry that you didn't leave sooner? If so, what stopped you?

6. Do you wish that you'd waited longer? If so, why didn't you?

7. Have you ever regretted a leave-taking? If so, what would you do differently?

no

8. What is the scariest part of being unemployed?

The unknown

9. How realistic are your fears?

10. Do you ever fantasize about leaving your current job?

Yes

11. What does your fantasy look like? How do you leave? Where do you go?

Leave on good terms, start a business.
Move to a new city, work in English

12. Have you ever burned any bridges on your way out the door?

Yes

13. How can you prevent yourself from burning any bridges now?

Stay calm and don't make it personal

(continues)

(continued)

14. What do you see as the greatest obstacle to leaving a job you dislike?

$

15. How do you plan to negotiate that obstacle?

Work at the same time, part-time

16. Before you make the decision to leave, are you sure that you've done everything in your power to fix your current situation?

not yet

17. If you're committed to leaving, how do you plan to support yourself during the transition?

x Not committed

18. How long can you afford to be unemployed?

x

19. Do you have a plan to bring in extra income? If not, can you think of how your skills might translate into temporary or freelance work?

x

20. If you'd never leave a job without having another one lined up, how do you plan to carve out enough free time to look for a new job?

Work fewer hours

21. Is there any danger that your employer might find out you're looking?

maybe

22. What do you think your employer will do if he or she discovers you're job hunting?

Take it personally

23. Does this scare you?

yes

24. Do you consider leaving an act of disloyalty? If so, would your employer show the same respect and loyalty to you?

yes, Maybe

25. Being completely honest with yourself, would it be better for you to stay where you are or to seek out a new position?

Not sure

26. Are you acting in your own best interests?

not sure

PART 3

The Path to Career Happiness

Chapter 9: Business Ethics: What's Your Bottom Line?

Chapter 10: Work/Life Balance: Making a Life While Making a Living

Chapter 11: Having Fun at Work

Chapter 12: We, Inc.: Working with Others or Starting Your Own Business

CHAPTER 9

Business Ethics: What's Your Bottom Line?

There is one way to achieve happiness on this terrestrial ball, And that is to have a clear conscience—or none at all.

—Ogden Nash, *I'm a Stranger Here Myself*

In Donald Westlake's novel *The Ax*, the central character, Burke Devore, is a 51-year-old paper executive who has been downsized. Although he is one of the best managers in the industry, there are simply too few jobs for too few people. So, he hatches a scheme to eliminate the competition. Pretending to be an employer, he places an ad in the newspaper describing the sort of job he is most qualified for and then proceeds to murder the top applicants. (Later he plans to murder the man who currently holds the job he covets.) His logic is clear:

> *Today, our moral code is based on the idea that the end justifies the means. And every single CEO who has commented in public on the blizzard of downsizings sweeping America has explained himself with some variant on the same idea: The end justifies the means.*
>
> *The end of what I'm doing, the purpose, the goal, is good, clearly good. I want to take care of my family; I want to be a productive part of society; I want to put my skills to use; I want to work and pay my own way and not be a burden to the taxpayers. The means to that end has been difficult, but I've kept my eye on the goal, the purpose. The end justifies the means. Like the CEOs I have nothing to feel sorry for.*

Devore is a fictional character. Though extreme, he also exemplifies the common workplace belief that "the end justifies the means": that in a dog-eat-dog world, it is necessary—and even commendable—to resort to the most venial tactics to vanquish your competitors. For Devore, the "enemy" was everywhere and everyone. Both the unemployed and the employed had become his enemies, desperation his psychological companion.

We like to think that, in the real world, things like this don't happen. But just the other day, one of the kindest, most intelligent men I know—a former physician—admitted to me privately that he used to have revenge fantasies about blowing up the building where his former employers still worked. What curtailed his fantasy was the recognition that, in blowing up the executives he loathed, he would also be taking down some innocent people.

Knowing how difficult his situation was, I wasn't surprised that this man might fantasize about revenge. (I would have been astonished, however, if he had acted out those fantasies.) Nonetheless, I found it profoundly disturbing that such a deeply nice and compassionate person could be pushed to the limits of such rage and desperation.

What he told me next disturbed me even more. Recently he had bumped into a former colleague who had been scapegoated by the same medical executives and, like my physician-acquaintance, had also lost his medical license. This man, however, wasn't just fantasizing about revenge. He had talked to a hit man about killing the executives who he blamed for destroying his career. Fortunately, he didn't follow through because the hit man was too expensive. But it's not as if this man has come to his senses and realized that hiring a hit man is wrong. He still regrets not having the money to hire the guy.

These stories—and others like them—are both instructive and disturbing. They reveal how deeply important a job can be in a person's life and how unsettling it can be to lose a job you really care about. Much like the end of an important relationship or the death of a loved one, losing a job can be a highly stressful and deeply traumatic event.

An FBI Agent Stands Up for Her Principles

The trauma of losing an important job is what makes people like Colleen Rowley—a woman who was willing to risk losing the job she had worked for all her life and, by extension, her career as an FBI agent, to stand up for her principles—that much more remarkable. When she was a kid, her favorite television show was *The Man From U.N.C.L.E.,* a spoof about two handsome agents whose mission was to save the world from evil. When she was in fifth grade, Rowley wrote to the show's producers asking if she could become the next agent from U.N.C.L.E. Recognizing a patriot in the making, the producers directed her towards the FBI, where the real special agents worked. Rowley contacted the FBI for information and learned that they did not hire women as special agents. But the determined youngster had the foresight to recognize that would change. She knew what she wanted to be when she grew up, and nothing was going to get in her way.

She took pride in being a pioneer, part of the first wave of women fighting to be taken seriously in the bureau's male-dominated, button-down culture. She worked her way up the ladder as an FBI lawyer—handling applications for searches and wiretaps, working organized-crime cases in New York City, and becoming, in 1995, chief counsel in the Minneapolis field office. She won a reputation as a highly disciplined professional who was opinionated, principled, and supremely devoted to her job.

All of this helps explain why she put her career on the line to blow the whistle on her beloved FBI in the wake of the terrorist attacks on our country. When she wrote a secret 13-page memo to the FBI revealing problems she had witnessed relative to the terrorist attacks, she was on a private mission to rescue her beloved employer from unethical practices, not a personal crusade to reprimand them publicly. But when the memo was leaked to the press, Rowley was thrust into the unenviable position of becoming front-page news.

Although it was easy for the rest of us (spectators) to be outraged at what the FBI had not done to prevent the terrorist attacks, I wonder how many of us would have had the kind of courage and integrity to do what Colleen Rowley did. I have a feeling not too many.

A Lack of Ethics

When advertising executives James Patterson and Peter Kim set out to "take the moral pulse of America," they discovered that most Americans are willing to do anything for money: abandon their families, change religions, lie, cheat, steal, or even murder.

Touching, isn't it? And it doesn't get any better. Take a look at some of the other results they documented in *The Day America Told the Truth* (1991, Prentice Hall):

- Lying has become part of our national character. Just about every one (91 percent) of us lies—regularly. In fact, most people can't make it through a week without lying. Some can't even make it through a day.
- When asked what changes they would make to better fulfill their potential, most people wanted to be richer and thinner. "Smarter" ran a very distant second. Becoming a "better person" didn't even make the rankings.
- When queried about the "sleaziest ways to make a living," car and insurance salespeople, Wall Street executives, real-estate agents, lawyers, and investment brokers ranked at the bottom of the moral sewer.
- There is only one clear moral authority and it isn't God, church leaders, teachers, or even parents—it's the individual. That is to say, nearly all respondents (93 percent) believe that they and they alone determine what is and isn't moral in their lives. And their actions bear this out. Most respondents (more than 80 percent) report that they've violated a law or an established religious rule because they thought the law was wrong.

So much for the wisdom of Aristotle, who believed that happiness was a function of virtue. He thought that if you worked hard to live as an ethical person, you'd feel good about yourself and your place in the community. Apparently, we prefer to live out the concerns of Jewish theologian Abraham Joshua Heschel, who remarked: "Suspect your neighbor as yourself."

In modern society we expect money to make us happy, so we pursue it with religious fervor. You'd never know from the way we exalt it that the "bottom line" is morally neutral. It won't get you into heaven. It won't make you a good person or a bad one (although how you make your living has a moral value). Masquerading as "realists," some people would have you believe that the whole world is a jungle where people watch out solely for themselves and only the cruel survive. A "bottom-line" mentality has become a convenient excuse to indulge predatory instincts. What happened to human evolution and the advances of civilization? Do we really want to go back to the jungle and kill each other for dinner?

The reality is that you can be a good person, live an ethical life, and still make lots of money. You can even use your power to accomplish some good. Principles and ideals aren't a luxury that you can't afford. They're a necessity you can't live without if you want to maintain your integrity amid chaos and corruption.

Although we laughed when actor Michael Douglas' *Wall Street* character Gordon Gekko declared that "greed is good," the line wasn't quite as funny when we are constantly reminded how deeply held this cherished belief runs within the business community. But don't look to the ivory towers of academia for better behavior. There you'll encounter people such as renowned historians Doris Kearns Goodwin and Stephen Ambrose, who have been accused of plagiarism, or Pulitzer Prize–winning authors inventing experiences in Vietnam and teaching them as biographical truth. Nor can we look to the hallowed sanctuaries of religion for comfort. Nothing has been more disturbing than the revelations of insidious and widespread pedophilia, child molestation, cover-ups, and corruption among the clergy within the Roman Catholic Church.

One powerful antidote to the deterioration of moral and ethical behavior in the workplace lies in the realm of character education. Character education is the deliberate effort to develop good character based on core virtues that are good for the individual and good for society. William Bennett, the former Secretary of Education, has become a well-known expert on the subject of character education. In his book *The Moral Compass,* he has gathered hundreds of stories, poems, and essays that illustrate virtues and values. The stories are arranged according to life stages and challenges from childhood through adulthood, including the challenges of perseverance, compassion, community, responsibility, and faith.

The Argument for Business Ethics

Arnold Hiatt, the former chairman of Stride Rite Corporation, sees public service as "enlightened self-interest." Citing his company's family-leave policy as an example, he notes that the program costs next to nothing financially. In human terms, however, it makes a statement of caring that creates goodwill with employees and motivates them to be more productive.

Unfortunately, most managers and business executives are more inclined to view profits—not people—as the lifeblood of their organizations. Profits are the master they serve. People only get in the way. That kind of thinking makes the phrase "business ethics" sound like an oxymoron and drives ethical people underground into the ranks of the alienated and dissatisfied, or out of the corporate sector altogether.

In many cases, the "bottom-line" rationale is a convenient excuse to operate "below the line" of human decency and social responsibility under the guise of good business practices. But is it really good practice to cheat your customers and exploit your employees for the sake of short-term profits? Apparently, a lot of people think so.

In *The Predatory Society* (1995, Oxford University Press), author Paul Blumberg examined deceptive business practices. His research uncovered 600 different accounts of consumer fraud (as reported by company employees), including the following:

- Retail establishments that mark prices up before sales.
- Gas stations that sell regular fuel as high-test.
- Auto mechanics who spray-paint old car parts and sell them as new.
- Pharmacies that sell generics and charge brand-name prices.

These incidents didn't even occur in the industries or professions that respondents to the Patterson and Kim study considered particularly unethical.

On the other hand, respondents did say they personally would do anything for money. Well, here's proof-positive they weren't kidding. In each and every case, profit motive was the force that drove businesses to consciously engage in fraudulent and deceptive business practices. The paradox for capitalists is that many profit-minded people apparently think the best way to make money is to trick consumers into thinking products are good quality. Why not actually produce and sell quality products, instead?

The spectacular cases make headlines when they're uncovered. In 1992, a once-celebrated Park Avenue attorney named Harvey Myerson was convicted of overbilling clients, including Shearson Lehman Hutton, more than $2 million. Besides ordering younger partners to inflate their hours (or else lose their jobs), he was happy to have Shearson pay his personal expenses large and small. These included family vacations, travel on the Concorde, and dry cleaning of his toupee.

Equally troubling is the well-publicized case of consumer fraud by two high-ranking Beech-Nut executives who were jailed and fined for marketing bogus apple juice as "100% fruit juice." In doing so, they tricked millions of unsuspecting consumer-parents into feeding their children what was mostly a mixture of beet sugar, apple flavor, caramel color, and corn syrup. They rationalized their behavior by saying that "everybody else does it, too." But of course, not everybody acts in a way that brings them a more than 350-count federal indictment.

Prior to this incident, these men were not criminals. Both were considered upstanding pillars of their respective communities. Unfortunately, they must have left their spiritual ideals and morals at the church door on Sundays, in order to wear the hat of "corporate patriot" again on Monday mornings. For that moral failing, they both went to jail, were fined $100,000 apiece, and racked up more than $2 million in penalties for their beloved Beech-Nut. They also destroyed consumer trust, shattered their own reputations, and ravaged the organizational spirit. These events didn't make employees proud to call themselves members of the Beech-Nut family.

When Co-Workers Do Wrong

It's easy to conclude as Lord Acton did that, "Power tends to corrupt, and absolute power corrupts absolutely." Yet eschewing power is hardly the answer. Powerlessness also corrupts. How else can you explain why all those junior partners who worked for Myerson were so willing to risk disbarment rather than activate some kind of personal moral compass? Obviously, they were more scared of losing their jobs than their licenses to practice law. So they caved in to the pressure to "do the wrong thing." But were there no other alternatives available to them?

Fortunately, the tide seems to be turning. After a series of corporate scandals (such as Enron, Arthur Andersen, WorldCom, Tyco, Healthsouth, and so on), there is more individual and collective support for those who dare to stand and fight. But the process can be arduous and emotionally draining.

Bob McIntyre was a Financial Consultant and Assistant Vice President with Merrill Lynch when he discovered that one of his supervisors made discretionary (unauthorized) trades in a client's account. Seeking to resolve the conflict amicably, he approached his supervising broker, who agreed (in theory) that what he was doing was incorrect and then continued the unauthorized trading. Seeing that the problem wasn't resolved in the client's best interest, McIntyre elevated his complaint up the food chain to his resident vice president, who instructed him that the matter was to "go no further."

However, McIntyre did press on. He drafted a complaint letter to the company's Ethics Hotline. Shortly thereafter, he noticed that he was being treated differently by management, and the company moved him to another division. After a six-week absence to attend to his mother during her terminal illness, his manager immediately placed him on probation, and then terminated him a few months later. McIntyre sued for breach of contract and prevailed. The NASD ordered Merrill to pay damages. However, he admits that the entire process has been a terrible ordeal for his family, and wonders whether he did the right thing.

"Truth be told, I felt as though I was compelled to take action," McIntyre says. "I just couldn't tolerate the length and breadth of the deceptive conduct toward an elderly client."

Ditto for a financial analyst who sued WorldCom Inc., alleging that the company instructed him to falsify financial records and then fired him for his failure to comply.

Given the massive business number of high-profile business scandals, Congress has enacted legislation to combat corporate corruption. The Sarbanes-Oxley Act includes measures to protect "whistle-blowers" who report financial wrongdoing, the first-ever that apply to employees at all public companies.

But that doesn't mean that employers won't retaliate. Should you choose to take the high road of ethical conduct, you'll still undoubtedly have to struggle to figure out how to save your job and still do the right thing.

There's Strength in Numbers

You don't necessarily have to take on the establishment single-handedly. Some people find strength and courage by banding together. When a high-ranking human resources executive ordered his benefits and compensation staff to "fudge their numbers" for the year-end audit, they collectively marched into his boss's office to register a protest. This team power play effectively put an end to his unethical demands.

Sadly, not every ethical professional can find power in numbers. A quality-control inspector for an outdoor-equipment manufacturer in California was upset by the lax standards her colleagues and supervisor were exhibiting toward certain products. This placed her in a practical and ethical quandary. She was uncomfortable with what she saw happening around her. Yet she feared reprisals if she went over her co-workers' heads and complained. And because her supervisor was one of the offending parties, she felt it would be futile to register a complaint with him.

Finally, she decided to rely on her sense of what's right to do, as well as her firsthand impression of the CEO as a fair-minded and responsive leader. Her instincts were good. The CEO took her complaint seriously and, without revealing the source of his information or jeopardizing her position, investigated and rectified the problem.

Doing an end run around the person you directly report to isn't always advisable. Before attempting it, you should evaluate your boss's boss realistically. If it seems unlikely that the executive will handle the problem discreetly, you might want to look for another, more direct solution.

An administrative assistant knew a member of her department was fudging expense reports, and it made her uncomfortable. Rather than ignore (and process) those reports, she pointed out to him that she thought he'd "inadvertently" made a mistake on his report. The word *inadvertently* was carefully chosen. It was her way of giving him the benefit of the doubt, as well as a way to correct the problem without having to admit that he'd been dishonest. It also sent a message that someone was watching. This encouraged him to keep more accurate expense reports in the future.

Fight Subtle Pressures

Unethical behavior doesn't always involve conscious fraud. Unconscious self-deception can fuel the fire, too. For example, many executives tend to view unethical behavior as "someone else's problem" rather than their own, says Oak Park, Illinois, psychologist Laurie Anderson. If they behave in a shady manner, they justify it as a necessary reaction to others' misconduct.

"Nobody ever owns up to being an unethical person," Anderson says. "It's everybody else who's unethical."

Rationalizing ethical slips isn't hard for people who must reconcile competing professional pressures. A prominent health-care attorney with a major Chicago law firm cites the situation in fee-for-service medicine, where overzealous physicians might rack up legitimate (but unnecessary) charges in the name of conscientiousness.

"Never mind what the client really needs," says the attorney. "Doctors and lawyers make those decisions for them. And sometimes those decisions are costly."

Excessive demands from higher-ups can also be a factor. For example, consider the timekeeping wars that go on in the legal world. I spent five years of my career as office manager for a medium-size general corporate law firm and was responsible for collecting and monitoring attorneys' time sheets. During my tenure, there was an ongoing push for associates to generate more billable hours, which in turn generated a silent feud among several of the associates.

All the firm's associates worked similarly long hours. However, one associate with some particularly "creative" timekeeping strategies made it look as if he was putting in more hours than his colleagues. One very meticulous, hard-working associate (who put in 10-hour days every single day) resented his colleague's timekeeping strategies, the partners' tacit agreement to look the other way, and the subsequent pressure it placed on him to work harder and bill more hours, too.

His personal integrity created a double bind. He didn't feel it was his place to blow the whistle on his colleague, nor did he wish to put in more hours than he already was. He certainly wasn't interested in padding his time sheets. But he worried that the partners would think he wasn't productive enough. He need not have worried. Working in the same office with him every day, it was impossible not to notice how diligently he worked.

As it turns out, both men became partners in the firm at the same time. Despite the conflict over billable hours, they were competent attorneys who achieved good results for the firm. But one was honest and capable, while the other was devious and manipulative.

It would be comforting to believe that, monetarily speaking, "crime doesn't pay." But that isn't always true. Sometimes, crime can be very lucrative. And just because the two Beech-Nut executives got caught doesn't mean that the next group of corporate thieves will suffer a similar fate. Besides, people who don't get caught don't make the six o'clock news.

The executives weren't even true bad guys (although they did show very poor judgment, for which they paid dearly). Their intention was to keep their company solvent and profitable. In their own minds, they probably genuinely believed that the "financial bottom line" of their company was more important than the law, fair business practices, or their own personal reputation. What they needed was a lesson in "Business Ethics 101," with special emphasis on personal integrity and social responsibility.

Find a Role Model

From a career perspective, if it doesn't bother you to "play dirty," it's up to you. As long as you confine your activities to legal ones, you can let your conscience be your guide. But don't make the mistake of thinking that you can't win playing fairly. Whoever said "nice guys finish last" most assuredly wasn't a nice guy. He obviously didn't have any appreciation for the financial value of such intangibles as consumer trust, employee loyalty, fair business practices, or quality service. You don't have to take him as your role model, either. Why not look for better role models with more character and integrity?

In government, former Attorney General Janet Reno stands out for her principle-centered leadership. Reno wasn't afraid to take tough stands and live with the consequences. As the first woman to hold the Attorney General's office, she blazed new trails for women. But beyond the politics of gender, her ability to lead with integrity brought a strength of character to the role that hadn't been seen since Bobby Kennedy held the office. When Reno became Attorney General, she announced that her decisions would be guided by one question:

What's the right thing to do?

Given the intricacies and manipulations built into the legal system, isn't that value-centered vision what you'd want from someone in that role? Reno didn't pussyfoot around issues or talk out of both sides of her mouth. She said what she believed and stood by those beliefs, even when things didn't turn out as she hoped. During the tragic and highly controversial Waco incident, in which several FBI agents and many followers (including children) of Branch Davidian cult leader David Koresh, were killed, Reno stood her ground when facing a scandal-hungry media and announced, "The buck stops with me."

More than anything, our workforce needs people who are willing to accept responsibility even when things go tragically wrong.

Defend Your Rights

Ethics isn't a set of moral positions; it's a process. It's a way of living in the world with integrity and self-respect. That means standing up for yourself when your rights have been violated and "doing the right thing" even when there's pressure to back down.

In the movie *Philadelphia,* Tom Hanks plays a corporate lawyer named Andrew Beckett who is fired from his senior associate's position, ostensibly for incompetence. In fact, however, Beckett is certain he was dismissed because he's gay and dying of AIDS. For Beckett, the ensuing lawsuit is as much a matter of principle as personal integrity. As his dying act, the once-successful attorney wants to restore his reputation and clear his name of any wrongdoing.

In a poignant scene, he asks his family's support for a lawsuit that will bring a great deal of public scrutiny and embarrassment to them. His mother shows her wholehearted support by saying: "I didn't raise my kids to sit in the back of the bus. You get in there and fight for your rights."

His mother's blessing notwithstanding, Beckett has a hard time finding an attorney willing to go against his powerful former bosses and defend his rights. As the movie unfolds, it also becomes a story of growing respect between Beckett and his homophobic lawyer, played by Denzel Washington. Gradually, Washington's character learns to see beyond his personal stereotypes and view his client as a whole, real person. Meanwhile, Tom Hanks' character holds other people accountable for their actions—in this case, lawyers who have broken the law.

There are real-life heroes who exemplify this spirit as well. If you're old enough to remember baseball great Hank Aaron, you might also remember the year he began inching toward Babe Ruth's home-run record (which he eventually broke). That year, Aaron also started receiving hate mail from die-hard Ruth fans who didn't appreciate that a black ballplayer was about to shatter their hero's records. The racist slurs surprised and disturbed him, but he never lessened his performance or his pursuit.

"It never slowed me down," Aaron told one interviewer. "It only made me stronger." Standing up for yourself and your beliefs takes strength and courage. But doing otherwise will take a serious toll on your self-esteem and reputation.

A laid-off investment banker in Chicago discovered that his former colleagues were disparaging him to prospective employers by speculating about nonexistent "performance problems." Rather than play victim, he took steps to safeguard his reputation and future. The banker called the firm's office manager and explained the legal and ethical dilemmas that his former co-workers' "loose tongues" and "false pride" were creating.

Although he never directly threatened a lawsuit, his tone and comments implied the possibility. His strategy of straightforward communication effectively put an end to the gossip that was damaging his career prospects. The office manager quickly sent off a memo making it clear that the big-mouthed offenders would be held accountable for their off-the-record communications.

Yes, there can be consequences when you act so aggressively. But standing by passively has its own consequences. What's the point of keeping your job but later being sent to jail? Or keeping your job and losing your license to practice your profession? Or keeping your job and losing your soul? Or even losing your job because you kept your mouth shut but the company got caught anyway?

Reshape the World

Writer Niko Kazantzakis believed happiness comes to people who wear the Reformer's mantle: those who work to remake the world in accord with their own beliefs and principles.

This appears to be the goal of New York attorney general Elliot Spitzer, whose office launched a full-fledged frontal assault on Wall

Street executives and the securities industry. Looking something like a white-collar Rambo, he barraged Merrill Lynch with subpoenas and carted off loads of incriminating documents. After making hundreds of internal ML memos public, there was no doubt that the company had engaged in one of the biggest pump-and-dump stock scams in history.

The company settled with Spitzer for $100 million. But if they thought they were done with him, they were wrong. Several months later, he captured Wall Street's attention again by revealing that Merrill Lynch analysts had been recommending stocks publicly while trashing those same companies privately in internal e-mails. The Spitzer probe turned up a series of explosive internal e-mails from Merrill analysts reflecting their disdain for the very companies they were recommending in public research reports.

Because the Merrill Lynch incidents turned out to represent standard industry practices, they were not the only losers in this game. Once they caved in, a number of other Wall Street firms admitted to the same unethical practices. A whole host of firms then coughed up $100 million (or, in some cases, $50 million apiece) for a grand total of $1 billion.

As a result of his effort, determination, and courage, Elliot Spitzer has spearheaded the most sweeping changes in the securities industry in over 50 years. And I have a feeling we haven't heard the last of him.

Trust Your Inner Strength

Our world cries out for courageous, compassionate, wise, and skillful leaders to provide vision and direction. Yet part of that moral complaint rings hollow. Like Dorothy in *The Wizard of Oz,* what many people really want is a parent to rescue them from the traumas of growing up.

L. Frank Baum's *The Wizard of Oz* is *the* allegory for our times, so relevant to this discussion that the tale bears repeating (if you've only seen the movie, you know only a small fraction of the story):

> *A cyclone rips through the Kansas prairie, where Dorothy lives in childhood bliss with her Auntie Em, Uncle Henry, and faithful dog Toto. The tornado tears the house from its foundation and carries it to a strange land Dorothy has never seen before. The countryside is beautiful and filled with strange sights, but Dorothy wants the safety of her aunt's arms. Without realizing that the ruby slippers she's wearing have the power to carry her home, she sets off down the Yellow Brick Road to ask the all-powerful Wizard of Oz to help her.*
>
> *Along the way, she meets up with the Scarecrow, who wants to travel with her to Oz to ask for brains. Poor Scarecrow believes that there's nothing worse than being a fool, and thinks he's stupid even though he's really just young and inexperienced. Already he knows two things for certain: to be afraid of lighted matches, and how little he knows. Some people might call that wisdom.*
>
> *The Scarecrow asks Dorothy to describe Kansas. When she explains how gray it was, he can't understand why she wants to return to such a dreary place.*
>
> *"That is because you have no brains!" Dorothy tells him. "No matter how dreary and gray our homes are, we people of flesh and blood would rather live there than in any other country, be it ever so beautiful. There is no place like home."*
>
> *"Of course, I cannot understand it," says the Scarecrow. "If your heads were stuffed with straw, like mine, you would probably all live in the beautiful places, and then Kansas would have no people at all. It is fortunate for Kansas that you have brains."*

After a while, their journey is interrupted by groans from a man made of tin, whose joints have become rusted from disuse. When they oil his joints, he sighs with satisfaction and thanks them for saving his life. Hearing of their mission, he asks to join them on their journey because he would like a heart.

The Tin Woodsman's story is a painful one. For much of his life, he was a woodsman who cared for his elderly mother. After his mother died, he fell in love with a Munchkin girl and wanted to marry her. But the girl's caretaker was an old woman who wanted the girl to cook and do housework for her forever. So the old woman got the Wicked Witch of the East to enchant the woodsman's ax, which made him cut off his own legs, arms, and head. The tinsmith replaced each part of the woodsman's body with a new tin part, but in the process, the woodsman lost his heart (and thus his love for the Munchkin girl). He stopped caring whether he married her or not.

The Tin Woodsman was proud of his new body, which no one could cut or hurt ever again. But rust was his enemy. He spent a year rusted in place, which gave him plenty of time to think. He decided that the greatest loss he suffered was his heart, because you can't be happy if you can't love, and you can't love without a heart.

While the Scarecrow and the Tin Woodsman debate whether it's better to have brains or a heart, Dorothy worries about what she'll eat, since she can't live without food. Hearing her concern, the Scarecrow uses the wits he doesn't have to gather nuts for her dinner from nearby trees.

Their next problem arises when they're "attacked" by a Lion who tries to scare them with his roar. When Dorothy calls his bluff and tells him he's a coward, he breaks down weeping. To his great sorrow, the king of the jungle lacks the courage to fulfill his destiny.

"My life is simply unbearable without a bit of courage," he says. So when the Lion hears of their journey, he decides to tag along and ask the Wizard of Oz for help.

As they travel companionably together, they encounter many problems and challenges. They conquer each obstacle by using the brains, heart, and courage they think they lack.

The Wizard, of course, turns out to be a fraud. But he is also a good man who manages to give Scarecrow a brain made from pins and needles, the Tin Woodsman a red cloth heart, and the Lion a magic potion for courage. But he doesn't have an effective strategy to get Dorothy home to Kansas. For that, they need the good witch Glinda, who knows how to use her powers wisely. First, she arranges to install Scarecrow, Tin Woodsman, and Lion in leadership roles throughout the kingdom where each can use their newly found talents to rule. Then she shows Dorothy how to use the power of her ruby slippers to return home.

Once you realize that Dorothy's journey is a dream, the story is easier to interpret. From a psychoanalytic point of view, the Scarecrow, Tin Woodsman, and Lion are parts of Dorothy's self that she's struggling to integrate. But she's terrified of separating from the safe world where her loving aunt and uncle care for all her needs. By the end of the adventure, though, Dorothy has grown in stature and become a more confident, self-assertive person.

Dorothy's lesson is a universal one: that we all need to separate from the powerful figures of our childhood to cultivate the wisdom, compassion, courage, and skill we need for our life's journey.

Dorothy needed the good witch Glinda to show her how to use the power she already had. This is what teachers, leaders, and mentors are really for. And despite what respondents to the Patterson and Kim survey may think, there are always real role models or heroes whose examples you can learn from and follow. You just have to cultivate the eyes with which to see.

The cry of our times is for more responsible participation. As Herbert Hoover believed: "We need to add to the three R's, namely Reading, 'Riting, and 'Rithmetic, a fourth—Responsibility." If you accept the responsibility to fulfill your destiny, you must cultivate all the skills of responsible participation: courage, compassion, wisdom, and initiative. Ignore your longing for a White Knight. You are your own White Knight now. Cultivate the leader within yourself and make that person someone who isn't afraid to care.

There are plenty of reasons to live an ethical life. But the very best reason to do it is for yourself. Integrity stands at the heart of self-esteem, and self-esteem is a crucial pillar of a happy life. If you can't respect yourself, you won't respect other people, either. And you won't like the life you're living, because you won't like the person who's living it.

When you get lost in the daily shuffle, tell yourself the Oz story. And remember the moral of the story: The Scarecrow, the Tin Woodsman, the Lion, and Dorothy all had the tools within themselves to achieve their deepest, most heartfelt desires.

Next time you head out the door for work, see how it feels to carry some compassion in your heart, some fire in your belly for the fight, and all the wisdom of your experience with you.

Business Ethics: What's Your Bottom Line? Thought-Starter Worksheet

1. How ethical is the organization you work for? (Circle one.)

Very   Somewhat   So-so   The pits

2. Where are they most likely to cut corners?

____

____

3. Do you generally agree with their values and priorities?

____

4. Have you ever been asked to do something that you felt was unethical? How did you respond?

____

____

____

5. Were you satisfied with the way you handled the situation?

____

6. Is there anything you should have done differently?

____

____

7. Have you ever ignored unethical behavior? Was it because you didn't want to get involved? Hate confrontation? Feared reprisal?

____

____

(continues)

(continued)

8. Do you believe that a certain amount of lying and cheating is normal and acceptable business practice?

___

9. If you insisted on more honest and ethical business practices, would it jeopardize your career mobility?

___

10. Would more ethical business practices interfere with your organization's ability to compete?

___

11. Do you believe that the financial bottom line is the most important consideration in any business?

___

12. Would you personally break the law to protect the bottom line?

___

13. Would you treat people unfairly to improve the bottom line?

___

14. Would you skimp on customer service to help your company's financial status?

___

15. Would you describe yourself as an ethical person?

___

16. Do your responses to questions 9 through 14 support your beliefs?

___

17. When you have an ethical conflict, whom are you most likely to consult?

___

18. How would you describe that person's character?

____

____

____

19. If you believe your organization suffers from bad business ethics, is there anything you can do to improve those practices?

____

20. Have you ever participated in an ethics training program?

____

CHAPTER 10

Work/Life Balance: Making a Life While Making a Living

There is only one success: to be able to spend your life in your own way, and not to give others absurd maddening claims upon it.

—**Christopher Morley**

Woody Allen likes to tell a story about the time he got kicked out of school for cheating on an exam. It was a metaphysics class and he tried to look into his classmate's soul.

You can't copy someone else's soul and call it the "right answer." But when it comes to finding a path to the Good Life, many people try. They follow a prefabricated career track others have created for them and hope it will lead to fulfillment. It rarely does. Everyone must find his or her own personal vision of happiness. The road to career satisfaction isn't always easy, though. Often, the initial task of thinking for yourself to determine your true goals can involve a painful separation process.

Some of the most difficult decisions involve the need to balance work and family. I can only imagine how difficult that balance must have been for George W. Bush's trusted advisor Karen Hughes who, prior to her departure from the White House, had been called "the most influential person" in Bush's political life. Despite her close ties to the President, she and her husband wanted her son to grow up in Texas, and she wanted to be there with him to watch him grow up and do all the things that an involved mom does for her kids.

Much as she loves politics and political life, Hughes believes that her most important responsibility in life is to be a good parent; so she chose to put her family ahead of her service to government. However, it was clear to everyone involved that, even from Texas, she would still be actively involved with President Bush and his administration.

Whereas many people struggle to balance work and family, others feel pressured to figure out what kind of work they really want to do for the rest of their lives. Glenn Hilburn is 34 years old. He has an undergraduate degree in business and nursing and a history of great success in two careers (Registered Nurse and IT manager). But he also discovered that "success didn't equate to happiness."

At first he enjoyed his work and was proud of his success. But then his definition of success began to change. With that change in vantage point came the realization that he was no longer happy with his work. Although he had been contemplating a change for nearly a year, he just couldn't find the right time. The longer he waited, the more depressed and lost he felt.

Says Hilburn: "I awoke on the eve of the anniversary of 9/11 and instantly wondered how many of the thousands of people that perished in the twin towers had been contemplating a change in career. Certainly, as a result of that tragic day, they would never have the chance to make that change. That morning was a life-changing time as I decided that I wouldn't continue the contemplation and risk losing my chance; so I went to work that morning and tendered my resignation, much to the shock and dismay of my superiors and colleagues."

His colleagues and superiors tried to dissuade him from this rash decision, but Hilburn was firm in his resolve. During the next three weeks, he was "floored" by how many people approached him to tell him how much they respected his decision and really wished they had the courage to take that same step. Fortunately, Hilburn had the financial resources and emotional strength to leave his job, even though he wasn't sure exactly what he wanted to do next. In a perfect world, it would always be so. But, in the real world, there can be other exigencies.

A partner in a prestigious Chicago law firm hated his job and wanted out. Sales appealed most to him, but his wife (who was also, coincidentally, a nurse) fought the idea. She feared a drop in family income and, more importantly, a loss of prestige. She loved the status she enjoyed as the wife of a high-powered lawyer, even if he hated his job. She wasn't a bad person. She didn't want her husband to be unhappy. She just wanted to go on living the life she was living. She wanted him to want that, too. He caved in to her pressure not to change. But the hopelessness of his situation depressed him terribly. Not only did he hate his work, he resented his wife for not supporting his desire to switch. It became a lose-lose proposition that made him feel as if he was "doing time" instead of living life.

It's easy to abdicate responsibility for personal life choices. But it almost never turns out right. Instead of living on automatic pilot, ask yourself where your work fits within the context of a whole life. Is it simply a way to keep bill collectors from your door? A vehicle for a lavish lifestyle? Or, perhaps, something more spiritual? Do you want your work to be the centerpiece of your existence? Or part of a more integrated lifestyle?

When was the last time you gave any thought to these kinds of questions? If you're like most people, it was probably back in college when the "meaning of life" was a more burning issue. After that, you got too busy to figure it out. Or perhaps you decided that the meaning of life is in the way you live it day by day.

Take a Break

Time is your most precious commodity. Like it or not, you probably give a major chunk of it to work. But how large a chunk do you really want to give? It's up to you, whether you realize it or not.

The Protestant work ethic has built a nose-to-the-grindstone, shoulder-to-the-wheel mentality into our collective psyches. This notion makes it difficult to justify taking time out (or off) to think about your goals and dreams. And as the pace in our technological society accelerates, it's becoming even harder to carve out quiet time for figuring things out. Yet "inner time" is crucial to good decision making. Without it, you never really gain enough perspective and self-knowledge to set your own course.

As director of the Center for Interim Programs in Cambridge, Massachusetts, Neil Bull spends a fair amount of time convincing people that it's OK for them to take time off to figure out what they want to do and where they want to do it. Mostly, he works with high school graduates to design yearlong sabbaticals that will better prepare them for college. To date, he has nearly 4,000 such programs to his credit. One of his greatest challenges is dealing with the protests of parents (usually the dads) who believe their kids will be led astray if they don't immediately move on to higher education. Despite their fears, every teen he's helped so far has gone on to college. So much for "father knows best."

Bull offers these kids "find yourself" time—a year to learn about the world and themselves. The programs include opportunities for adventure and discovery as well as play, and bring the teens greater confidence and newfound direction. It's a year that most adults also desperately need but seldom get. Bull remembers doing verbal battle with former baseball commissioner Peter Ueberroth over the built-in values of a success-driven culture. Although he didn't convince Ueberroth (who is troubled by health problems) to give up the chase, he has convinced others to come around to his way of thinking.

When he was top dog for Merrill Lynch & Company, Don Regan approached Bull with an intriguing assignment: plan sabbaticals for a pair of high-ranking, 60-something Merrill Lynchers to reward them for their 30 years of devoted service. Regan (who was later hired and fired by the Reagan administration) hoped the sabbaticals would help the veteran executives bridge the gap into retirement and help them think more creatively about their options.

When I asked Bull why people needed help planning their time off, he responded bluntly: "Most people have no imagination or training. Unless you tell them exactly what to do and how to do it, they can't find a ZIP code in southern Illinois."

"Come on," I said. "We're talking senior executives here, not high school kids."

What Bull said next was fascinating: "Most people are terrified to take time off. The fear factor is so rampant that when they let go for even a few weeks (not to mention months), they feel like they're writing their own obituary."

The worry is that if your employer can get along without you for several months or a year, management might conclude that they can do without you forever. If you're in the office 60 to 80 hours a week, you can protect your territory better. This logic makes some sense. However, are you sure you really want the territory you're so fiercely defending? Or are you just protecting it because it's yours? If you let go and allow the company to make do in your absence, you might be surprised at what happens to you. Once out, many people express no desire to ever go back.

Thinking of a Permanent Vacation?

A facilities manager in Boulder, Colorado, needed to detoxify from his 60-hour work weeks, so he took advantage of his company's personal leave-of-absence program. Suddenly, he had time to bike, play tennis, and do volunteer work. The manager liked his more-relaxed lifestyle so much, he never returned. Instead, he took early retirement and started his own company.

In his 22 years at Rohm and Haas Company in Philadelphia, researcher John Lopuszanski has seen many employees come and go. But the one who stands out most in his mind is a senior chemist who was given officially sanctioned time off to finish her Ph.D. She was even guaranteed a job when she returned. Rohm and Haas was true to its word. The chemist completed her education and she did come back. But she didn't stay very long. "At the time, there weren't a lot of female chemists with Ph.D.s. It didn't take long for her to realize how marketable she was and move on," says Lopuszanski.

In another scenario, a commercial banker in San Francisco negotiated a six-month personal leave to complete her fine-arts degree. After returning to the bank as promised, she discovered that her heart (and now her degree) were really in photography. She soon quit to become a photographer full time.

If you're considering stepping away, getting the go-ahead from your employer isn't the main problem, says Neil Bull. Instead, it's whether you can give yourself permission to take time off. He believes that we've all been afflicted by John Calvin and the Protestant work ethic, and personally curses him every morning for making people feel guilty every time they take a break.

Time away can be truly restorative. Even if you like your work, it can help you reconnect with yourself and the aspects of your life you find important. Damona Sam, a 40-something counselor and assistant professor at the Community College of Philadelphia, would have to agree. A year off from her job, where she's one of two counselors assigned to 5,000 students, was just what she needed to recover her health and a piece of her sanity. Although the school would only agree to pay her half-salary (plus full benefits), the psychologist jumped at the chance to relax and recoup.

Sam had her first child while still in the process of writing her doctoral dissertation. However rewarding, both activities took a real physical and emotional toll. Indeed, her first priority was to get her health back. Her second goal was to get reacquainted with her husband and spend more time with her son. Beyond that, she took her leave one day at a time, hoping to get in touch with her own needs and desires.

Five months into the sabbatical, she noticed that her experience of time had changed dramatically. "I feel like I'm living in a different time frame," says Sam. "I was always a 'human doer.' Now I spend time just 'being.' It's like a gift from the heavens to take time off—a gift I thank God for every single morning." Sam's "being" time is the existential time she takes for herself to walk along the lake, watch the sunrise, or jog slowly through the park. It's time that's governed by inner rhythms and unrestrained by schedules or clocks.

You can probably identify with Sam's time-management dilemma. On a typical workday, she must juggle a full plate of family and career responsibilities. Although she accepts responsibility for her commitments, they leave her drained and exhausted. She partly blames the advent of computers and other labor-saving devices designed to make us all more efficient. They increase our expectations and push us to do more, rather than use any time saved for leisure and relaxation, she says.

Starting a Whole New Life

Time off can also become the impetus for a dramatic lifestyle change. When Arkansas attorney Frank Mackey took a summer leave of absence from his corporate law firm, it was with the intention of exploring the Chicago job market. Specifically, the 60-something Mackey wanted to know whether he had a chance of cracking the commercial acting market. Within six weeks, he had his answer. He returned to Little Rock just long enough to sell his partnership in the firm and pack his bags.

Like many established professionals, Mackey was longing for more than a job change. He wanted a whole new life—a chance to start over in a completely different place doing something entirely new. It was a decision that came with a very high price tag—but not one that he regrets. Mackey's wife has a well-launched legal career of her own in Little Rock. For her, Chicago winters aren't desirable. Neither is the idea of starting over. A short stint with a commuter marriage didn't prove satisfying, either. So, the Mackeys decided to go their separate ways.

Other couples fare better. Connie Evans and her husband Craig were long-time employees of Ameritech in Chicago. She was a secretarial supervisor; he was an engineer. Together, they earned a comfortable living, owned an attractive suburban home, and were able to save for the future. The only problem: Connie was totally miserable. Although she did her job competently, she hated the office politics. She longed to work in a more comfortable, creative environment. She desperately wanted out of corporate America, but didn't know where she wanted her career to go. One weekend, when she and Craig were driving through the Wisconsin countryside, the answer shouted out to her. They'd buy a bed-and-breakfast inn and move to the country.

They began to research the B&B market, talking to owners, scouting locations, and getting a feel for the finances. The idea only grew on them. Then, Connie started spending her Sundays driving to various Wisconsin inns to check them out. Soon, she found and fell in love with the Port Washington Inn, a lovely, affordable B&B just 30 minutes outside Milwaukee.

They realized that they could afford it if Connie cashed in her 401(k). But they knew they couldn't live entirely on profits from the inn. So Craig approached his boss about a transfer and got the green light for his job to move to Milwaukee.

After their bid on the inn was accepted, the rest of the wheels were set in motion. They fixed up their house, put it on the market, and sold it in about two months. Connie gave notice at her job and, in a remarkably short time, they were gone.

Connie took to her new career like the proverbial duck to water. She's always been a homebody who loves to entertain, garden, and cook gourmet meals. Even dreaded chores such as laundry and housework don't particularly bother her.

Personally, I was a little skeptical about this blissfully perfect solution. I wanted to check it out for myself. So one Saturday after giving a workshop in Milwaukee, I took the half-hour trek to spend the evening with Connie and Craig. Port Washington is a small town on

Lake Michigan, which means there's some good, steady tourist trade to sustain it. It's also a true 30 minutes from Milwaukee, making it an attractively short commute.

The house is beautiful: carefully restored and lovingly attended. Connie's care and handiwork are everywhere. Every room is decorated in its own theme. No detail has been missed—from fancy soaps and creams in the private bathrooms to candies on the nightstand. On weekends, they prepare gourmet breakfasts for their guests; and on weekdays, they set out fresh-baked goods. To do so, Connie spends a fair amount of time with her nose buried in cookbooks, experimenting with new recipes.

As a host and hostess, they're warm and hospitable. Your wish is their command. Even their dog, Woody, looks totally content. And well he should, since he's treated like a veritable prince: well-fed, well-exercised, and much loved.

It isn't perfect. Nothing is. They have to work hard to keep the B&B operating. It has taken effort to ingratiate themselves to the community. And Craig still works at Ameritech, when he might, perhaps, prefer to join Connie at home. It's a very fair compromise, though. More than ever before, they love the life they're living.

Less Is More?

A pervasive hunger for a simpler, less stressful life showed up clearly in a *Time* magazine survey of 500 professional adults. Just consider the following:

- 69 percent of the respondents wanted to "slow down and live a more relaxed life."
- 61 percent agreed that it takes so much effort to earn a living that it's difficult to find time to enjoy life (that's why you need to find a way to enjoy the way you make a living).
- 89 percent felt it was important to spend more time with their families.
- 56 percent wanted more time for personal interests and hobbies.

Many of these would-be slow-trackers hunger for country or small-town living. However, it's easy to overidealize that lifestyle. Rural life isn't typically an easy answer; more often, it's an adventure that should be reserved for people who come from pioneer stock.

Life on the Slow Track

A new breed of career trendsetters is making life in the slow lane look mighty good. In *Downshifting* (1991, HarperCollins), business journalist Amy Saltzman identifies five different models you can use to get more control over your work and life:

1. **Backtrackers** arrange for their own demotions so that they can have more time and less stress.
2. **Plateauers** intentionally stay in place. They turn down promotions because they don't want the increased pressures of more responsibility.
3. **Career-shifters** transfer their skills to less stressful fields.
4. **Self-employers** go solo to have more control over their work hours and location.
5. **Urban escapees** opt for more hospitable, relaxing environments in the country, small towns, or the great outdoors.

In the movie *Baby Boom*, Diane Keaton is a successful marketing consultant in New York City. A star on the rise, her relentless ambition fuels her workaholism. Not the least bit introspective, her only signs of discontent are revealed in her irrational desire to read and clip real-estate ads for country homes.

Keaton's life changes dramatically when she inherits a baby from a distant cousin. Soon, Keaton discovers the perils of combining single motherhood with a fast-track career. Good child care is tough to come by and time is at an absolute premium. When she can't give her career the single-minded attention she once did, an ambitious young executive (in the form of James Spader) moves in on her territory and grabs her prized account. As her partnership opportunities fade into oblivion, Keaton is offered a new role on the "slow track."

It is a blow to her pride and she can't agree to it. Suddenly, that country home looks mighty appealing. So the impulsive Keaton quits her job, buys a house from a real-estate agent sight unseen, and moves to the country with her baby.

Picture this: Here's a woman who's always lived in a luxurious high-rise and whose attention and energy have been focused entirely on climbing the corporate ladder. Within a few days, she's living in a run-down house, playing mother to a child to whom she's grown attached, and living an isolated life in a small town where the natives aren't exactly welcoming her. The winters are cold, and her home needs major repairs at a time when she has no income.

She needs a job. But there isn't much call for marketing consultants in her community and she doesn't know how to do more everyday labor. Eventually, she finds a dormant entrepreneurial drive inside her that spawns the start-up of Country Baby, a gourmet baby-food company targeted toward baby-boomer parents like herself.

Because the movie is a Hollywood fairy tale, Country Baby becomes a spectacular success. Keaton's former employer contacts her with a $3 million buyout offer and, to sweeten the deal, offers to keep her as the CEO of Country Baby. Only then does she realize that she doesn't need or want "the rat race" anymore. She can make it on her own, even if it means turning down a cool $3 million. Of course, there's a new lover in the background fueling Keaton's desire for a comfortable relationship and a life where love does, indeed, conquer all.

Moving Someplace Else Isn't Always the Answer

Ignoring the movie's spectacular finale, Keaton's small-town experience does actually parallel that of many big-city folk who underestimate the difficult challenges that come with the transition to a supposedly simple life. Most of the time, you don't just waltz into a ready-made lifestyle; you create it with your own vision and skill.

"What people don't realize is that there's a difference between a summer vacation and a lifestyle," says Sharon Schuster, editor of *Re Careering Newsletter* in Lake Bluff, Illinois. Schuster, who's been studying these changes since 1986 when she was downsized out of a public-relations job with AT&T, says geographic cures are like comfort foods.

"When people are reeling from the emotional trauma of losing a job, they're looking for comfort, fun—something to make them feel good," she says. "But the reality is that these aren't always easy life choices, either."

After several ratings guides recently touted Fayetteville, Arkansas, as the darling of relocators, Schuster tracked down several urban refugees who migrated there in search of a better life. One was former Chicagoan Linda Ray, who moved down at age 50. To her dismay, Ray discovered that the town's economy didn't greet every transplant with open arms. She found that there wasn't much of a market for her broad communication skills in such a small community. It also didn't help that there was considerable competition for lesser positions from university students and faculty spouses. She'd never imagined it would be so hard for her to get a toehold. She was forced to fall back on the proceeds from the sale of her house to support herself.

Ray saved her career by launching her own marketing services business, eventually narrowing her focus to advertising. By joining the local chamber of commerce and volunteering for several community activities, she slowly integrated herself into the town and achieved the less-frenetic pace she had so desired.

Despite her early financial difficulties, she doesn't regret her decision to leave Chicago and is pleased with the new life she's created in Fayetteville. But she warns prospective transplants to be realistic about the employment opportunities. "It could take a good solid year to get established," says Ray, "so you'd better have a full year's living expenses set aside before moving day."

To minimize potential disillusionment, Schuster recommends investigating what it would be like to live elsewhere before packing your bags. Use your vacation time to check out the job market, talk to locals, and determine just how feasible your plan is.

"A little reality-testing can go a long way," says Schuster. For example, she says that if you plan to start a business, "you'd better make sure there are enough resources available to you. A phone and a fax may not be enough." Top on her list of "musts": a decent postal system, a good library or research institution, and a regional airport.

Alternative Work Arrangements

With so much change in the workplace, there are also opportunities for creative and resourceful people to invent new ways of working. Three of those concepts are addressed in this section: telecommuting, part-timing, and job-sharing.

Telecommuting

Some savvy professionals mitigate the financial risk of moving to a more relaxed town by negotiating to take their current jobs with them. If you can't arrange a transfer, telecommuting might be a viable option. To carve out such an arrangement, though, you need three things: job responsibilities that are truly portable, an employer who doesn't want to lose you, and the ability to remain motivated and self-disciplined without traditional office structures.

Telecommuting isn't a license to play hooky on someone else's dollar. It's an alternative work arrangement that buys you a lot more flexibility, but depends on your ability to produce results from afar.

A computer-software consultant was transferred from his New Orleans home to Washington, D.C. It did wonders for his career, but it wasn't that great for the rest of his life. After three years, he was terribly homesick for his friends. He submitted his resignation, intending to return to New Orleans to look for a new job. But because the company valued him greatly, they suggested that he set up an office in his home in New Orleans and remain on their payroll. He accepted eagerly: He loved his job; he just loved New Orleans more.

The arrangement proved win-win. Not only does he love the freedom of working at home, he's amazed at how much he actually accomplishes in a day without the distractions of office life.

Solutions like these aren't easy to come by. Nor are they dumb luck. They result from on-the-job brilliance. When you're great at what you do and your bosses appreciate your work, you almost always have more options available to you.

Going Part-Time

Obviously, brilliance alone won't get you permission for an alternative work arrangement. You'll also probably have to do some skillful prodding of your employer. When *Wall Street Journal* columnist Hal Lancaster interviewed Rosemary Mans, she discussed her desire to carve out more time for her family without destroying her career credibility with San Francisco–based Bank of America. It took a full year of convincing to get the bank to allow her to become a part-time vice president of flexibility programs. She admits it was a hard decision and a hard sell. Flexible work options—such as a part-time schedule or telecommuting—are generally considered career poison. If you try this approach, you'll probably be considered less committed to the organization, less serious about your career, and a nuisance to management (because you're never there when they need you).

Still, if you want to go ahead, there are ways to sell your employer on the idea. For example, you can say that as a part-timer, you'll be more focused and productive during the hours you work. You'll be able to provide better customer service because you'll have more energy for it. You might even save your employer some money on benefits (although this isn't a great advantage for you).

Job-Sharing

Job-sharing offers another viable way to balance work and family responsibilities without burning yourself out or destroying your career path. The concept of job-sharing involves two people sharing one full-time job by working at different times of the day or on different days. *Working Woman* magazine recently applauded Laura Palumbo Meier and Loriann Meagher for their career savvy in lobbying Xerox to let them share a sales-management position in their Lexington, Massachusetts, office.

No manager had ever asked to job-share before. But the former sales rivals (each were 13-year veterans) convinced their bosses to let them try. Now they're among the highest-ranking Xerox executives to successfully share a job.

For those who are interested in more flexible options, Lancaster recommends the following guidelines:

1. **Don't just ask for favors.** Put together a realistic proposal that outlines the performance goals and objectives you'll meet under your new schedule.

   Meier and Meagher drafted a detailed, 30-page proposal and revised it three times until it adequately addressed the concerns of their immediate boss and the human resources department. In it, they spelled out their schedules, day-to-day tasks, and plans for managing the sales team.

2. **Make your manager your best friend.** Your boss needs to trust you and feel comfortable with your working arrangement.

   Before Meier and Meagher ever submitted their plan, they talked it over with their boss, Janice Orlando Duplisea. A working mom herself, Duplisea empathized with their concerns and challenged them to convince her they could really make it work. When the two demonstrated their commitment to the idea, Duplisea became the real catalyst.

3. **Stay abreast of developments.** When you're out of the information loop, it's easy for things to fall through the cracks.

   Meagher and Meier make it their business to share information so that neither one of them will fall from grace. They have a formal communication system to update each other, as well as a flowchart of how issues will be resolved.

   It's difficult to anticipate every problem that will occur under a more flexible schedule and to have systems in place to resolve them. Thus, you need to have people you trust to keep you informed, or else you run the risk of obsolescence.

   Meier and Meagher were smart enough to understand that they each had different strengths and weaknesses. They divvied up their responsibilities and schedules accordingly. Example: Since Meagher has an extensive background in leasing and financing, she's responsible for writing up the sales forecasts. Meier, who's stronger at personnel issues, handles the lion's share of employee reviews. But before they finalize and sign off on any documents, they go over them together.

4. **Make sure that home and family commitments don't completely outweigh work priorities.** If you don't adjust your schedule to accommodate true office emergencies, you'll quickly send the message that (a) you're not a team player; and (b) you can't be counted on. After that, don't be surprised to find your credibility seriously in jeopardy. You'll be left out of important meetings, miss out on information (large and small), and generally feel alienated from workplace events.

   Meagher and Meier make a point of showing their dedication to the workplace team. Although they're both working moms with family commitments, they also make sure they look like ambitious, goal-oriented professionals who take their careers equally seriously.

When you deviate from tradition, you'll undoubtedly encounter some skeptics and critics who prefer conformity to imaginative problem-solving. You can follow their tired prescriptions for success, or take your cues from someone like Robert Shaw, conductor of the Atlanta Symphony Orchestra. At the 20th anniversary of the Kennedy Center, Shaw was one of six performing artists honored for a lifetime of achievement. Said Shaw: "The only crescendo of importance is the crescendo of the human heart." Another musical great gave similar advice. In a conversation between pianist Vladimir Horowitz and Arturo Toscanini, the great conductor cautioned Horowitz to take his own counsel: "If you want to please the critics, don't play too loud, too soft, too fast, too slow."

Pay Attention to Yourself

You can devise a zillion creative solutions for conflicts between your work and personal life. But they all require some introspection. Change comes from the inside out, so you have to pay attention to yourself. As Mary Nissenson Scheer says, "You don't need someone else to tell you when you're in love. You trust your instincts." In her opinion, most people don't trust their gut enough. They look to others to hand them ready-made answers that seldom (if ever) work. Until you learn to heed the signal from your own heart, it doesn't matter what others want and think you should do.

Peggy Simonsen, president of Career Directions in Rolling Meadows, Illinois, tells a fable about what happens to people who listen too much to others' dictates.

> *Two men were taking an ass to market for sale. Since they had many miles to travel, they took turns riding on the animal's back. First, one man would ride while the other walked. Then, they'd reverse roles.*
>
> *Halfway through the journey, they stopped for a drink. As they rested, an old friend passed by and stopped to visit. "Look at that poor animal, "the friend said. "It's totally*

worn out. While you two ride in luxury, that poor creature is getting heat exhaustion."

The men agreed. The animal did look tired. Refreshed from their break, they decided to walk the rest of the way. For the next few miles, they trudged down the long, dusty road.

Soon, they bumped into a local merchant who was also bringing his wares to market. The merchant eyed the ass skeptically.

"If you want to get any money for that animal at all," he said, "you'd better carry it the rest of the way. Otherwise, it won't be worth a plugged nickel."

The two men were tired, but the merchant did seem to have a point. So they scrounged around in the woods for tree branches that'd be sturdy enough to support the animal's weight. They tied its hoofs to the makeshift poles and hoisted the upside-down animal gingerly onto their shoulders, trying to distribute the weight evenly.

Trudging ever more wearily along, they arrived at a bridge stretched across some whirling rapids: the last leg of the journey. As they negotiated the steep incline, one of the men suddenly tripped on a small stone and toppled sideways. He lurched against the railing, taking the poles—ass and all—with him. Unable to stop the momentum, the other man also lost his balance. Helplessly, they watched the ass collapse into the water and drown.

When I heard the tale, Simonsen was speaking to a packed house of college students who were waiting expectantly for her conclusion.

"What do you think is the moral of the story?" she asked.

Silence, except for a few uncomfortable giggles.

"Listen to everyone's advice and you will surely lose your ass."

Start on the Right Foot

If your job doesn't allow much calendar and clock freedom, you might find yourself fighting for every moment of free time you get. It helps if you can clarify your needs (and your employer's expectations) soon after you're hired. Then, after you've agreed on a schedule, you won't have to justify your actions every time you leave at 5 p.m. or don't come in on the weekends. Even if you can't get much schedule flexibility, you can still set realistic limits to your workday. As Emerson said: "If you can't be free, be as free as you can.

Five Career Fantasies

Everyone dreams about what they would do if they didn't have to work. How many of these common career fantasies have you caught yourself yearning for?

Hitting the Road

Jack Kerouac fantasies of hitting the open road. Getting behind the wheel of a car—or better yet, an 18-wheeler—and being out in the wild blue yonder, making your own plans, no one looking over your shoulder, no office politics to worry about.

Taking a Big Risk

Living a life of adventure: racing cars, climbing mountains, fighting fires, catching crooks.

Being More Creative

Writing, painting, acting, drawing. Taking some creative risks. Being a creative person. Developing more creativity.

Tahiti, Inc.

Moving somewhere fun like a tropical island.

Make a Contribution

Doing something that's not "just" about making money.

Former FBI Director Louis Freeh had the good sense to negotiate some free time into the terms of his employment agreement. Freeh at first declined the $133,600-a-year job, citing disruption to his family life as his primary concern. When his wife prevailed on him to reconsider, he said he'd take the job under one condition: He promised to work diligently for the FBI, but he also planned to reserve quality time for his wife and two sons.

The White House agreed and the appointment moved forward. But it's unlikely that Bill Clinton anticipated just how seriously his FBI director took his commitment to his family. Late one Friday, Freeh was notified quite suddenly that he was expected at a Saturday-morning White House meeting. Sorry, he replied. Unless it was a national emergency, his Saturday morning was already booked. He'd promised his sons that he'd attend their basketball game, and he intended to keep his word.

Of course, you aren't Louie Freeh. But you can learn an important lesson from his modus operandi:

1. Be very clear about your needs and priorities.
2. Be very, very good at what you do.
3. Make sure your employer knows just how good you are.
4. Insist that your employer meet your needs.

Most people don't change their lives all at once. It's an incremental process that takes constant self-evaluation, careful goal-setting, and self-directed action. You must persist in the face of obstacles and criticism. Succeeding in your new life requires clear thinking to understand that reality isn't always as idyllic as you might expect. But it's not an impossible dream. And it can be well worth the effort. Just the other day, one of my more inspired life-changing clients (who took early retirement to pursue other career goals) startled me with an incredible statement: "I feel as if I'm living in the center of a chocolate cake," she laughed. "Everything around me is so sweet."

Work/Life Balance: Making a Life While Making a Living Thought-Starter Worksheet

1. Do you wish that you had more time for yourself?

   Yes

2. Where do the greatest demands on your time come from?

   work

3. Can you enlist more support to help you meet your responsibilities? From whom?

4. How good are you at setting limits?

   pretty good

5. What happens when you say "no"?

   quiet

6. How good are you at asserting your own needs?

   so-so

7. How can you improve your negotiating skills?

   Think win-win
   Believe that I deserve what I want

(continues)

(continued)

8. Do you wish that you could work fewer hours?

Yes

9. Have you ever considered working part time?

Can't

10. How do you think your employer would feel about part-time hours?

Fine

11. Do you worry that people will think you're not serious about your career?

NOT really.

12. Is there any precedent in your company for job-sharing?

bah.

13. Is there anyone you'd like to share a job with? Who?

14. Can you think of any benefits to your employer of a job-share arrangement?

15. Would you like to work from home more?

16. Do you have the kind of job responsibilities that lend themselves to home-based work arrangements?

____

17. Do you think your employer would object to your working from home part-time? If so, why?

____

____

____

18. Can you experiment with alternative work schedules to determine how feasible they really are?

____

19. Do you ever fantasize about a whole new lifestyle? If so, what does your dream life look like?

Less work, more play.

More spontaneity. More friends.

More travel.

20. Have you ever lived in a small town? If not, what do you think it would be like?

a bit close for comfort.

Slower pace

____

21. Do you know any urban refugees who moved from the city to the country? If so, what has their experience been?

____

____

____

(continues)

(continued)

22. Can you see any negatives to rural or small-town living?

23. Have you ever considered a sabbatical or an extended leave of absence?

24. How do you think your employer would react to such a request?

25. How would you spend a year off?

Self-improvement → more exercise
→ more cooking
→ a retreat
→ travel

26. What do you think would happen to your career if you took a year off?

27. Would that scenario be so terrible?

CHAPTER 11

Having Fun at Work

Take risks and smile. Have some fun—it's not against the rules.

—Hap Klopp, *The Adventure of Leadership*

So, off your duffs, couch potatoes. Pick up your camera. Tune up that instrument. Sharpen those woodworking tools. Get out those quilting needles. Lose yourself in the flow of active work and play.

—David Myers, *The Pursuit of Happiness*

Many people associate fun with the frivolity of youth or relegate their playtime to their leisure activities. The assumption is that laughter, fun, and play are immature, unadult, and unprofessional when, in fact, humor and fun can help individuals cope with stress, crisis, and change.

Before they wrote their book *301 Ways to Have Fun at Work* (1997, Berrett-Koehler), David Hemsath and Leslie Yerkes were already convinced that fun at work was the single most important characteristic of an effective and successful organization. They saw direct links between fun-filled work and employee creativity, productivity, morale, satisfaction, retention, customer service, and other critical factors that determine business success. To prove their point, they conducted an international survey to collect relevant real-life stories of what people are doing to create fun workplaces.

But I didn't need to read their book to appreciate their truths. In a so-called "24/7" work environment where people are often stretched to their emotional and physical limits, fun and the energy and enthusiasm it creates are critical to both success and satisfaction.

Laughter Really Is the Best Medicine

Denise Driscoll would love to be a stand-up comic. Although she can't afford to take the financial risk, that hasn't stopped her from making laughter part of her job. Driscoll is an oncology nurse in Chicago. You might not think her job would offer much opportunity for humor. Attending to cancer patients is obviously serious business. But she knows that beyond being good fun, laughter is also good medicine. To encourage healing through fun activities, she established one of the first "humor carts" in a Chicago hospital. But that doesn't mean you'll find her romping wildly through the ward with a bag of magic tricks and a passel of jokes stashed in her hip pocket. When it comes to humor, timing is everything. Driscoll might love laughter, but she never uses it as a replacement for compassion and caring. Rather, it is a way of showing love.

It would be easy to view this 50-year-old woman as a child who never grew up and, indeed, there is a youthfulness to her personality. But she had to teach herself and the people around her how to have more fun in the midst of illness and crisis. That theme is echoed in the movie *Patch Adams* (based on the real-life story of Dr. Hunter "Patch" Adams), an unconventional but highly determined young doctor who is convinced that laughter really is the best medicine, a belief that often makes him look foolish and nearly gets him thrown out of medical school, but is very popular with many of his patients.

If you're like most adults, the wear-and-tear of everyday life has probably taken away some of your gift for laughter. As a child, you were likely to have laughed more than 100 times a day. Sadly, research shows that by age 44, most people are down to less than a dozen mild chuckles daily, if that. Life as a grownup can be pretty much of a downer.

Denise Driscoll would like to change those numbers. "Humor is like verbal aikido," she says "and you can find it in everyday life." Denise is part of a burgeoning group of professionals who are dedicated to promoting the benefits and use of therapeutic humor.

Steve Wilson was already a well-established professional with a successful career as a college professor and psychologist when he founded the World Laughter Tour. Through the creation of laughter clubs, the World Laughter Tour promotes awareness of the benefits and techniques of therapeutic laughter, which they believe can promote both personal wellness and world peace. The WLT's motto is "Think Globally, Laugh Locally." The task of creating an "epidemic of world laughter" is a daunting one. But you can rest assured that Dr. Wilson and his WLT contingency are having a wonderful time trying.

Although some professionals might look askance at this lighthearted approach, there's plenty of good research to support their beliefs. You might be familiar with the story of the late Norman Cousins. While an editor of the *Saturday Review* in 1964, Cousins was treated for a crippling collagen illness that was excruciatingly painful and supposedly irreversible. Refusing to give up, Cousins had a movie projector set up in his hospital room so that he could watch "Three Stooges" movies and Alan Funt's memorable television series, *Candid Camera*. Cousins discovered that 10 minutes of genuine belly laughing created an anesthetic effect that allowed at least two hours of pain-free sleep. Eventually, he managed to laugh his way out of the hospital and a very serious illness.

Besides any physiological advantage, laughter can also help you to maintain (or regain) your perspective, increase your emotional resiliency, and cope better with stress. But you might have to provide context occasionally to make sure others don't get the wrong idea. For example, the human resources director of a psychiatric hospital in the Midwest was upset that patients were not adhering to hospital regulations. When she complained bitterly to the medical director about it, she was astonished to hear him laugh at her concerns. Seeing her chagrin, he hastened to explain: "We're treating psychiatric patients here. If they didn't have problems, you and I would be out of work." By mixing humor and common sense, the medical director was able to gently remind the HR director that she shouldn't expect patients to be trouble-free or to behave in a totally rational manner. Knowing your audience—as the medical director did—is the first step toward successful service delivery and your own mental health.

Laugh in the Face of Fear

Using humor to diffuse tension is a survival skill that was practiced adroitly by members of the medical team on the popular TV series *M*A*S*H.* Actor Alan Alda's Hawkeye Pierce is especially memorable for his ability to crack terrific one-liners under pressure. Of course, he also had the benefit of great writers.

This was not true for the real-life Capt. Alfred Haynes, a 33-year veteran with United Airlines. One hour into a flight from Denver to Chicago one July afternoon in 1989, his plane's rear engine exploded, requiring an emergency landing in Sioux City, Iowa. Haynes was trying to maneuver his DC-6 with 296 passengers aboard safely onto the ground using only the engine thrust. As he did so, he was in contact with an air-traffic controller who advised him that he was cleared to land on any runway. At that point, Haynes was just hoping he wouldn't end up in a cornfield. So he laughed and said: "You want to be particular and make it a runway?"

When you're able to call forth humor under such dire circumstances, it provides an important emotional outlet, allowing you to retain your sanity. As Abe Lincoln once said (paraphrasing Byron), "I laugh because I must not cry."

Finding Everyday Fun

The ability to maintain that kind of heroic grace under pressure is often admired yet seldom practiced. Even in far less threatening situations, many people have trouble lightening up and finding a bit of humor in the moment. Especially at work, people often prefer to keep a tight rein over all emotions.

When Lou Ella Jackson first became a trainer, she was aware of research indicating that people learn better when they're having fun.

Taking the information to heart, she realized that she'd have to lighten up her presentations to make them more effective. She admits it wasn't easy. "I came out of the financial industry, which has a reputation for being very staid," says Jackson, the former president of the Chicago chapter of the American Society for Training and Development. "I was very comfortable with my serious professional persona, when suddenly I was confronted with the idea that I needed to make my seminars more fun."

The first time around, Jackson really had to psych herself up to be playful with seminar participants. "I told myself that it didn't matter if I looked stupid because I'd never see those people again, anyway," she says. The ploy worked. The workshop was so successful (and so much fun for everyone) that she never returned to her more formal style. Even in her career-transition workshops, where many of her students are reeling from the trauma of job loss, she finds that making room for laughter and play eases their pain and anxiety. Picture her tossing a soft baseball around the class to "get the ball rolling," or tattooing gold stars to participants' notebooks in exchange for a good answer to a tough interview question. By the end, many participants have enjoyed experimenting with job hunting in the workshop so much that they can't wait to actually do it, says Jackson.

A Chicago psychologist goes one step further. When she and a co-trainer rolled out a new career-development program for human resources professionals, the zany pair actively looked for ways to introduce fun into their sessions. Otherwise, they knew the 12-hour study days would be too intense. One time, she brought a jack-o'-lantern to class as a Halloween treat. It was filled with candy bars, which she gave out as rewards for correct answers. More than a satisfying snack, the candy added an element of friendly competition that made the learning fun. Then there were the squirt guns that participants were allowed to use on anyone in the group who babbled too long. "So maybe the competition wasn't always friendly," the psychologist laughs. "But it was always lively. There was an energy in the room that helped us get through some pretty dense material."

A former high school English teacher for the Chicago Dramatists Workshop, Gerissa French never forgets to bring a playful spirit to her work with students. Knowing how silly they can be, she's less inclined toward games and tricks. For her, fun means stimulating discussions on a subject she feels passionately about: literature. French works hard to bring out the same excitement in her students. She sees herself as something of an orchestra leader; her goal is to bring forth the very best performance from each of her student-performers. To do that, she knows she must inspire them to become absorbed in the class.

"I'm an excitement junkie," says French. "I crave the stimulation of discussion—the way students get involved with the work. The last thing I want to do is stand up there and pontificate. To me, that's boring." French doesn't tolerate classroom slackers. "If you can't get excited about the topic of a paper, write about something else," she tells her students. "I don't care if you choose great works or not. Just choose works you really love."

When students aren't excited about a topic, it shows and their papers are mediocre, she says. But when they're enthralled by a subject, the results can be magical. She remembers one such moment when a lackadaisical 11th grader's writing really came to life. The assignment was to write about a woman artist whose life or work you really admire. To her surprise, this student chose an obscure 13th-century European composer whose monochromatic style approximated a Gregorian chant. It was hardly the kind of role model you'd expect from an adolescent boy. But clearly, the work itself had captured his imagination and called out to him. Because he was so excited about it, he was able to express himself more clearly and effectively than he ever had before. It was an empowering moment for him, a poignant teaching experience for French, and a vivid example of why it's so important to find ways to add enthusiasm, energy, and plain old fun to your job.

Gerissa French knows two great ways to accomplish that. First, try to enjoy the people you work with; and second, involve yourself in projects that truly interest you. Both these strategies will add entertainment value to your day. However, you don't have to be an entertainer to increase your fun quotient. You just need a friendly attitude, a playful spirit, energy and enthusiasm, and a sense of humor.

From Play to Success

When Taco Bell president John Martin decided to shift his company's focus from operations to customer service, he encouraged his employees to come out from behind their work areas and interact more with the customers. "We wanted to make it more fun for everybody," he says. The strategy improved both the quality of workers' lives and his company's bottom line, as evidenced by Taco Bell's 38-percent increase in profits that year. Basketball coach Pat Riley learned a similar lesson about the relationship between fun and success. When Riley loosened up practices and the team started having fun again, they also started winning ballgames.

The urge to enjoy yourself is innate. When you make the effort to enjoy yourself at work, you're doing what comes easily and naturally. You're also increasing your chances of success.

As a customer, you can tell when the people who serve you are enjoying themselves. Usually, it makes you want to do business with them again. At Southwest Airlines, keeping customers entertained is such an important part of flight attendants' duties that a sense of humor is now part of the job description. To test that trait, candidates are asked to describe their most embarrassing moment and how they got out of it with humor. Flying Southwest from Houston to Chicago, I experienced that lighthearted touch firsthand. A flight attendant burst into an impromptu rendition of "Sweet Home, Chicago" as the plane touched down on the runway at Midway Airport. Her performance was followed by a startled moment of silence; then the passengers burst into a spontaneous round of applause. As we left the plane, everyone seemed to be more relaxed and happy for the experience.

Then there's Scott Alyn, the purpose-driven CEO of Something Extra, a Fort Collins, Colorado, greeting-card company. His stated business objective is "to bring lightheartedness into the world through my products." Every aspect of his firm reflects that goal. Even the credit and collection department exudes a playful spirit. For example, instead of the usual stern invoice, customers with past-due accounts are sent a package of spaghetti noodles in a cello bag with a card attached that reads, "Pasta Due" or "Please pay-a-uppa or we breaka your noodle." The mailing label on his company's shipping packages has a picture of a gopher in tennis shoes with a package under his arm and a caption that reads "Gopher Express." Not surprisingly, the company has exceptional customer relationships.

When you delight your customers like that, you improve word-of-mouth and, in turn, your business's sales. You also improve your own state of mind and make your co-workers and bosses happy, too.

Adding Humor to Your Life

1. Surround yourself with people who have a sense of humor.
   a. Make friends with the funniest people at work and at play.
   b. Stay connected with friends who make you laugh.
   c. Encourage others to laugh and be funny.

2. Entertain yourself with humor.
   a. Read funny books.
   b. Collect cartoons.
   c. Collect tapes/videos/books that make you laugh.
   d. Go to comedy clubs.
   e. Watch funny movies.

3. Lighten up at work.

a. Collect jokes and funny stories to tell your co-workers.

b. Post new cartoons and humorous anecdotes in the break-room.

c. Plan social events that are fun for everyone.

d. Learn to laugh with others and at yourself.

4. Make laughter a habit.

a. Consciously look for the humor in every situation.

b. Never miss an opportunity to make another person smile.

c. Set smile goals for each and every day.

d. Don't worry. Be happy.

Peter Lind, who heads up the research and development team for Ben & Jerry's in Waterbury, Vermont, also brings a playful spirit to his work. During factory tours, his laboratory is in full view. Rather than pretend he's working diligently every minute, Lind acknowledges tourists' presence by holding up a sign that says, "We're professionals. Don't try this at home." What else would you expect from a former chef and actor who responded to a help-wanted ad that listed "playing with your food" as a prerequisite for the job?

Bob Basso, the president of Light Management Associates, a motivational speaker in Hawaii, and coauthor with Judi Klosek of *This Job Should Be Fun!* (2000, iUniverse.com), believes that productive play is the key to success. This is especially true now, he says, when so many of us are expected to work harder, longer hours for the same money. Rather than let your performance slip because you're discouraged about diminishing incentives, you can enjoy your work and make it its own reward.

Herman Cain, the CEO of the Godfather's Pizza chain, describes fun as the key to self-motivation. "Fun helps remove the barriers and allows people to motivate themselves," he says.

Career consultants, however, often have trouble convincing the dissatisfied professionals they counsel to lighten up. Says Lawternatives' President Cheryl Heisler, "A lot of people can't get past the idea that you can have a 'real job' and still have fun working," says Heisler. "Unless they're bored out of their skulls, they think it isn't real work."

Howard Campbell agrees. As an independent outplacement consultant in Oak Park, Illinois, Campbell fights an uphill battle to convince clients that their first objective should be "finding somebody to pay you to do what you're good at and enjoy." Their second objective, says Campbell, is to "find an environment where you feel comfortable to be yourself." His views are usually greeted with skepticism. "Yeah. Right. I should be so lucky," they tell him. But luck has little to do with it. Self-knowledge, a positive attitude, and determination are the core requirements, not luck.

Campbell knows of what he speaks. For 20 years, he worked at traditional corporate jobs for which he was ill-suited, including 11 years as a human resources manager with Packer International, a high-tech medical firm in Bellwood, Illinois. Yet he describes himself as "the world's worst administrator." Because he wasn't much interested in the paperwork end of his job, doing it competently required a lot of energy.

"If you don't enjoy your work, how can you expect to be good at it?" asks Campbell. Heisler agrees. Like Campbell, she spends a fair amount of time convincing clients that it's OK to get paid for having fun. In her experience, people usually succeed much faster when they enjoy their work because it comes more naturally to them. The key, says Heisler, is to know what makes work fun for you. In other words, define the terms of your enjoyment. "Fun is unique to the individual," she says "Finding your niche is critical."

For her, nothing is more pleasing than when she receives an unexpected call from a television or radio producer to book her on a show, or when a reporter asks for advice for an article. Whereas others eschew the limelight, she embraces it. Vocationally, it's an emotional high that gets her adrenaline pumping.

What Delights You?

Every profession has its playthings. By choosing subject matter that delights you, your day will automatically go more easily. Physicists play with mathematical formulas. Architects love form and space. Writers love to play with words and ideas.

Like Peter Lind, Karen Messina-Hirsch loves to play with food. As the president and founder of Food Performance in Wheaton, Illinois, Messina-Hirsch makes food the center of her professional life. It's a focus that had its roots in early childhood. Growing up in a small Italian community in New Jersey, she has fond memories of working side by side with her mom in the kitchen. Apparently, she also had early signs of talent. As an eighth grader, she won a local contest for her innovative German chocolate cake. By high school, she already knew she wanted to work in a test kitchen.

College brought food-service, dietetics, and business-administration degrees along with early kudos for her culinary skills. She managed a bakery at Oklahoma State University in Stillwater and then moved on to the test kitchens at General Mills in Minneapolis, never once doubting that food was the career for her. She's since gone out on her own as an independent consultant. In her mid-forties, she returned to school to pursue a culinary arts degree at Kendall College in Evanston, Illinois. Because she's already 25 years into a successful food career, others questioned her need for that education so late in the game. Yet she has an endless curiosity for her subject matter and a tireless energy for learning the skills.

Although no job is perfect, Messina-Hirsch often labors with joy. Her career has seen many variations, but food is always at the center of the enterprise. Still on her horizon: She might write a cookbook or host a cooking show. She admits to admiring Martin Yan of the popular TV program *Yan Can Cook* for his incredible cutting methods. "He's like a virtuoso pianist," she says. "He probably spends hours just practicing his knife techniques."

Although her family and friends sometimes think she's a little too dedicated, her time spent drumming up and testing new recipes is not only work, it's also play. You can call it a busman's holiday, but she's thrilled to spend her days off in the kitchen puttering with new dishes. To her, it's all grist for the mill—experience she can apply later in her work with corporate clients. This is a woman who knows that work can and should be a celebration of talents, not an exercise in tedium.

Surrounding yourself with activities you love increases your potential for satisfaction. But it isn't always easy to find ways to integrate your interests and skills into your everyday work life. It takes energy, effort, and a willingness to take chances. Heisler cites the example of a general-practice attorney. The lawyer's first passion is for horses, but she wasn't sure whether and how to convert her passion into a livelihood. So she started slowly, working as a part-time riding instructor on weekends to see whether she was on the right track. She was. Today, her life as an attorney is far more tolerable because she knows it's almost over. Day by day, she's working toward the time when she'll be able to buy a horse farm in northern Wisconsin. Sound like fun?

Admittedly, hobbies make high-risk career choices. At the same time, they practically guarantee you enjoyment. The real question is, how much do you want to risk on the possibility of happiness? Although you might envy people like Messina-Hirsch and the future horse-farm owner, their spark is the result of finding and following a personal dream. Messina-Hirsch thinks fun—as a by-product of work—becomes more important as you age. At 54, she's aware that time is precious and wants to make sure she enjoys every minute she can. That's why she's always looking for new ways to expand her knowledge, develop her skills, and enjoy herself.

New York career counselor Judy Rosemarin has come to a similar conclusion. At 25, Rosemarin was determined to make people take her seriously. When she was 35, she was still intent on pursuing that goal. By the time she was 45, though, she recognized that she was trying too hard and decided to lighten up. "Once I realized that I was taking myself too seriously, I relaxed and let go," says Rosemarin. "And guess what? That's when people started to take me seriously."

Perhaps you need to stop working so hard to gain respectability and take your own happiness more seriously. Or, as some would say: Lighten up and live a little.

Take on a New Adventure

If you're on the lookout for new adventures in living, there are role models trailblazing new paths all around you. Ann Krcik was a rock climber who dreamed about quitting her marketing-operations job to work with fellow adventurers in the great outdoors. She made the leap by launching a Salt Lake City, Utah, firm that represents "extreme" athletes, signing them up to appear in commercials, and as models and motivational speakers. "I wanted more freedom to climb than my two-weeks-a-year vacation," says Ms. Krcik, whose work now takes her to mountain ranges throughout the Western states. "It was a fantasy I made come true."

Perhaps you remember the Reebok commercial where two real-life brothers put their sneakers to the bungee-jumping test (only to discover that the Reebok-less brother failed the jump)? Those two infamous bungee-jumping brothers once were average Americans with traditional corporate jobs. Peter Kockleman was an engineer (whose boyhood hero was Evel Knievel). His younger sibling, John, was a computer consultant. In 1987, they saw their first bungee jump on the TV show *That's Incredible*. They decided to try it themselves by jumping off a 140-foot bridge at Don Pedro Reservoir near Yosemite. The thrill got them hooked. Soon, John quit his job and convinced Peter to do likewise. "Come on, screw security," John said. "Screw stability and upward mobility. That's not what you're on earth for—to sit there and be calm, to sit there and die slowly."

The Kocklemans went on to become the kings of bungee jumping by founding Bungee Adventures, a California firm that arranges others' leaps of faith. Since they began their company in 1988, they have rigged over 50,000 bungee jumps in the U.S. and set two world records for the longest bungee jump. They have jumped from cranes, bridges, balloons, parachutes, helicopters, and hotel lobbies. They have manufactured equipment, appeared in commercials, and performed stunts in television commercials and movies. Talk about giving up security for a life of adventure!

Improve Your Social Life

Most fun work has a number of "wow" factors. Besides the intrinsic interest and excitement, it can also create more dynamic personal relationships. Denise Driscoll's friends look forward to telling her new jokes. The future horse farmer makes new acquaintances at the stable and takes old buddies riding with her. Karen Messina-Hirsch entertains friends with her culinary skills, and they join her in the kitchen for impromptu lessons. One Thanksgiving Day, she suddenly hauled her carving knives out of the car and, on request, carved the hostess's veal breast, to the oohs and ahs of an admiring audience. Heisler's new friends are media personalities. But her long-standing pals love to turn on the radio or TV set and find her friendly face smiling out at them.

Contrast those experiences with that of the vice president of a small cosmetics manufacturing firm in Chicago who finds his work tedious. He's so glad to shut the door on it each night that he never wants to discuss it after hours. This part of his life is increasingly closed off from other people. At parties and family gatherings, he assiduously avoids the topic of his business. When someone brings it up, he changes the subject. In the process, he makes himself more unhappy. He constantly hungers for more creativity, intellectual stimulation, and people contact.

He feels trapped and unhappy. Because he works in a family business, he doesn't feel he has the luxury of changing jobs or careers. So he tries to build more stimulation into his daily life with extracurricular activities. As a jazz composer, he's partly successful. But that doesn't entirely compensate for the 9-to-5 doldrums. To overcome them, he drew one of his zanier relatives into the family business to help with some sales and marketing responsibilities. By sharing the duties with a livelier, more outgoing person, the vice president found a way to enliven his own day and feel less lonely at his job. Although it's an imperfect solution (he still doesn't like his work activities), it has alleviated a piece of the problem.

When your job has humdrum responsibilities and you feel you can't leave, you can still lighten the load by working more joyously with the people who share that burden. For example, when Lou Ella Jackson first worked as a bookkeeper for a financial institution, her entire department worked together to alleviate the boredom. In addition to holding weekly breakfasts, they'd create contests to see who could "balance the most often" or "make the least errors." The sociable competition stimulated more productive and efficient work. It also enabled them to feel more involved and connected to each other.

Even if your organization frowns on employees having fun with customers, you can still try to have fun with your co-workers. You might not think that being a documentation specialist would be a real hoot. Yet one such expert enjoyed herself immensely while working with a marketing team to introduce a new product worldwide. She admits that her package-labeling responsibilities weren't particularly sexy, but the opportunity to work with so many diverse and dynamic professionals was "a real kick." To this day, she remembers that project as great fun. And although she's since moved onward and upward, she misses working with people who really knew how to have a good time together. What she doesn't realize is that she can exert more influence on her surroundings. She can initiate more fun-filled projects and activities herself instead of waiting to react to others.

How to Nurture a Sense of Humor

- Start your day with a new assumption: "This day will be fun."
- Amuse yourself while you're getting dressed or making breakfast. Wear something colorful or throw together an unusual treat.
- Kibbutz with the doorman, bus driver, cab driver, or train conductor. But keep your chatter to three minutes, tops.
- When reading the paper, go to the comics section before tackling the news.
- Share a funny story with the person sitting next to you on the bus or standing behind you in line for coffee.
- Play a comedy tape on your Walkman.
- Make fun of people at the health club for being flabby and out of shape. Then, fall off the treadmill yourself.
- Laugh about your commuting misadventures with the receptionist when you walk into work.
- Pretend to throw your telephone messages in the garbage.
- While planning your workday, look up and smile at the cute photographs of family and friends you have around your office.
- Buy a Joke-a-Day calendar and share the knee-slappers with co-workers.
- When calling people, ask to hear some good news.
- Look for opportunities to laugh in meetings with your customers, clients, co-workers, and boss.
- Bring yummy food to work.
- Speaking of food, go someplace new for lunch.

- During boring meetings, look at the participants and think about which actors would play them if this were a television sitcom. Who would win the role of your boss, your secretary, and, most importantly, you?
- Use humor in memos and letters to trusted customers and friends.
- At dinner, review the day's events in an amusing way to your dinner companions.
- Use your imagination whenever possible.

"The highest form of humor is laughing at yourself," says Denise Driscoll. "The greatest thing about it is that you never, ever run out of material."

Having Fun at Work
Thought-Starter Worksheet

1. When was the last time you really had fun at work?

____

____

____

2. What were you doing?

____

____

____

3. What made the experience fun? The activity? Or the people?

____

____

4. If it was the activity, was it an extracurricular event or part of your normal workday?

____

5. Do you generally enjoy your job activities?

Yes and no

____

6. Is there anything you can do to make your job duties more interesting?

____

____

____

7. Are you a creative person who enjoys building or making things? If so, is there a way for you to be more creative at work?

____

____

____

8. Does your job challenge you to grow and learn new things?

____

9. Are there any projects you can initiate that you'd find particularly interesting and challenging?

____

____

____

10. Who do you most enjoy working with? Be specific.

G

____

11. Why do you find them enjoyable?

Easy to talk to; positive attitude; empathic; team player; respectful and supportive; professional; giving

12. What do your preferences say about you?

____

____

____

(continues)

(continued)

13. Would you describe your co-workers as "fun to work with"? What about your customers?

Often.

14. Describe your organizational culture.

Friendly but fragile.
Hierarchical like an octopus – gravitating around one person.
Dysfunctional family

15. Do you feel that you belong there? Why or why not?

Yes and No.
appreciated → not really being myself or sincere

16. Do you have any personal resistance to having more fun at work? Are you afraid, for example, that a more lighthearted approach will make you look unprofessional?

Maybe

17. Do you believe that having fun with your customers can increase their satisfaction with your company's products and/or services? Why or why not?

Yes, but sometimes it's hard to achieve

18. Do you believe that having fun with your employees can improve team spirit and productivity? Why or why not?

Sure but to a limit

19. Do you view yourself as a fun-loving person?

More or less.

20. Do you derive more enjoyment from playing with things than with people?

Yes

21. Can you think of small ways to introduce more enjoyment into your workday?

Accept people as they are.

22. How do you feel about friendly competition?

okay

23. Do you find that you don't have time to have fun?

Sometimes

24. How much time does fun take?

good point

CHAPTER 12

We, Inc.: Working with Others or Starting Your Own Business

Our success will be measured by the answers to four questions: First, were we truly men of courage? Second, were we truly men of judgment? Third, were we truly men of integrity? Finally, were we truly men of dedication?

—John F. Kennedy

Nobody works entirely alone. Sooner or later you must interact with customers, colleagues, co-workers, bosses, and/or customers. That is why the ability to communicate and get along with other people can make or break a career. Sure, there are people who seem to be successful despite the fact that they are jerks; but you can't count on being one of them. To ensure your own success—and satisfaction—you need to develop successful people-management skills.

Managing Your Boss

One of the most important career skills is learning to manage upward. Much as I hate to admit it, it's true that flattery can get you somewhere with your boss (but only if you really mean it). Randall A. Gordon, a University of Michigan psychologist who reviewed 69 studies on the topic, concluded, "ingratiation shrewdly employed will get you ahead. If you have two people who are both competent at what they do, but one is really good at schmoozing…the one likely to get the raise is the schmoozer. It gives you the edge."

For those of you who aren't good schmoozers, there's no reason to get discouraged. Instead, you need to develop a solid, mature work ethic and relationship with the people you report to.

Boss-Management Guidelines

Here are a few guidelines to keep in mind:

- **Manage expectations and priorities.** When you receive a new assignment, make sure you know what is expected of you.
- **Solicit feedback.** Don't be afraid to ask for feedback about your work. It's better to know the truth, even if the truth (as your boss sees it) isn't completely flattering.
- **Keep the lines of communication open.** Share information with your boss and look for ways to make him/her look good.
- **Don't gossip.** Regardless of how you feel about your manager, don't share your negative feelings with others in the company. The things you say in private have a way of making themselves known to the wrong people.
- **Be a team player.** Although it's important to protect your own needs and rights, there are also times when you will need to put your department or company's needs in front of your own. Knowing when to take a stand is part of the art and skill of being a good team player.
- **Manage conflict and disagreement.** When you're feeling unfairly criticized, discuss your concerns rationally with your boss in a nonconfrontational way.
- **Build trust.** A key element in managing your boss is building trust in the relationship by being trustworthy. Make every effort to maintain honesty and dependability by honoring commitments and deadlines. Your positive example will impact not only your boss, but also others around you.

- **Sell your issue.** To get what you want in your organization, you have to ask for it, and you have to sell your boss on the issue. This isn't manipulation, but a legitimate set of techniques to make it easier for your boss to understand and accept your ideas. Don't expect your boss to understand your issue automatically. Learn how to present it, and, where appropriate, involve other individuals in the selling effort. With some bosses, you'll be more successful selling your issue in private versus trying to convince them in a public setting. And of course, pay attention to your timing, making sure you present the issue when other more pressing issues are not consuming your boss's attention.
- **Focus on what you can change.** Although you might not be able to control your boss, you can control your attitude. A shift in attitude, or the way you see things, can change your level of job satisfaction.
- **Give positive reinforcement.** Everyone in an organization needs support. You don't have to be a schmoozer to praise and appreciate another person's accomplishments. Some experts even suggest that the most important objective for employees is to appear supportive of their bosses. Empathize with your boss and express appreciation when it can honestly be conveyed. This will help your boss do his or her job better. And making your boss a better boss has obvious ramifications for you as well.

Now that I've given you all these great guidelines for managing your boss, I'm willing to admit that some bosses are simply impossible to work for. They are mercurial, dominating, overbearing, and irascible. Nothing is more anxiety-provoking than knowing that your job security and career advancement depend on your relationship with someone like that. Should that happen to you, the key is to expand your power base both within and outside the organization by building relationships with other people. This can help you make a lateral move within the organization or find a new job in a different company.

Building Strategic Alliances

So, how do you build strategic alliances within your own company without antagonizing your boss? Bob, a test engineer, solved this career dilemma by offering to represent his division in an interdepartmental forum. This looked like a win-win scenario. His overworked boss was happy to let Bob shoulder this particular responsibility. And Bob was able to develop greater exposure and credibility in the organization. After giving a presentation at one meeting, Bob was approached by another manager and offered a job in another division, which he graciously accepted. Although his boss was sorry to lose his employee, his boss never knew how much Bob disliked him. As a result of this strategy, Bob was able to salvage his career with the company without burning any bridges with his former boss—another form of a win-win situation.

Would a Lateral Move Help Your Career?

Making a lateral move from one position to another within the same company (that is similar in pay and status) is often an effective way to stimulate career growth. According to Beverly Kaye, a Pennsylvania-based career expert and author of *Up Is Not the Only Way* (2002, Davies-Black), moving across divisions in your company can mean adding contacts. It also can help you gain perspectives you might never have gained by simply moving up. In many cases, lateral moves solve relocation dilemmas for employees who do not want to move to new locations.

When you choose to make a lateral move, however, you must also be aware of the perception that this creates. You don't want to send the message that you are not a team player or that you are not ambitious. On the other hand, it makes perfect sense to tell a new manager that you are interested in expanding your knowledge and skills. This demonstrates that you are a motivated and enthusiastic learner. But it's still up to them whether they have the time and patience to train you to work for and with them.

Before making a leap to a new department where you will be performing different responsibilities, you need to make sure that your new boss understands that there will be a learning curve for you before you will be able to contribute fully. Don't be afraid to clarify expectations before making the leap into a new arena.

Escaping a bad boss is not the only (or even the best) reason to make a lateral move. When organizations grow slowly or are cutting back, lateral movements are an important career option. A sideways move can provide you with an opportunity to expand your base of skills and knowledge in a particular area, or across different functional areas of the organization. If you have a good relationship with your boss, you should be able ask for his or her advice and help in making a job change within the company. Perhaps your boss can refer you to some other area of the company. Changing departments can give you the breadth of experience that will be critical for success later. Lateral moves increase your portfolio of marketable skills and widen your network of personal contacts. If you want to learn new skills, seek the stimulation of new colleagues, relocate to a different location, or transfer into a faster-growing area of your organization, you could benefit from repositioning yourself by seeking a lateral move.

Finding a Mentor

Having a mentor can be critical to the growth and success of your career. But it can very hard to find the right person to mentor you. So, what can you do to find someone to nurture your talents and career?

The first key is to "know yourself." The more you know about your own talents, personality, strengths, and weaknesses, the better able you will be to define what kind of mentor you need to help guide your career.

In some cases, mentoring relationships develop naturally out of school, workplace, or personal relationships. For my friend Adam, a fortuitous relationship with his teacher, Kim, became the foundation of a lifelong mentoring relationship with Kim and her husband, Joe.

But this wasn't a relationship that Adam sought out. It was one that literally fell into his lap. Because most of us can't count on that kind of luck to guide our progress through the workplace, we have to be more proactive about seeking out mentors.

Blaze Konkol is a good example of someone who does this quite naturally. When Blaze decided to change careers from management consulting to counseling psychology, he was particularly interested in combining business and psychology. After hearing me speak at a graduate seminar, he took the initiative to contact me, at first for career advice, and later about the possibility of working together. Because Blaze views me as someone who has knowledge and contacts in the field he wishes to enter after graduation, he has very proactively solicited my advice and been open about his desire for me to mentor him. I, in turn, have learned a great deal from him and appreciate the assertive way in which he manages his own career and seeks out the connections that make the most sense to him instead of allowing himself to become alienated.

Blaze found me himself. But if you don't know anyone personally whom you might want to mentor you, you can ask for referrals from friends and colleagues in order to tap into other peoples' networks. The clearer you can be about who (or what) you are looking for, the easier it will be to get connected to the right people.

Keep an open mind about who your mentor or mentors might be. Because a mentor is someone who can help you grow in an area that is important to you, you might be looking for more than one person. Perhaps you need one mentor to help you with your writing and another person to help strategize your career moves. Or you might be looking for a role model.

Mentoring can be a two-way street rather than just a top-down experience from manager to staff or employer to employee. Senior staff who feel hopelessly out of date can benefit from the savvy and expertise that younger co-workers can bring to the table. One marketing communications executive developed a reverse-mentoring program where the younger employees who have grown up on computers match up with older workers who aren't as techno-savvy. Joining youthful know-how with senior influence can foster strong collaborations along with skill development.

Reverse mentoring went mainstream when former GE CEO Jack Welch insisted that several hundred of his top managers hook up with younger employees in order to learn about the Internet. Since that time, reverse mentoring has become a popular managerial strategy to manage intergenerational differences, understand younger consumers, and generate new ideas.

The hardest part of reverse mentoring is getting the teacher to be patient and articulate enough to teach the mentee. Younger mentors can also encounter some resistance from their senior-level mentees, who might be concerned about looking incompetent or getting too chummy with the staff. One solution to that dilemma is to use outside mentors from local colleges, universities, youth groups, and so on who are not part of the org chart.

Mentoring Exercise

Make a list of five people whom you admire. They can be famous people or people who stand out in some way for you by way of their character traits, qualities, talents, accomplishments, personality, and so on.

1. ______________________________

2. ______________________________

3. ______________________________

4. ______________________________

5. ______________________________

(continues)

(continued)

Identify five reasons why you admire each of them; be as specific as you can.

Person 1: ____________________

1. ____________________
2. ____________________
3. ____________________
4. ____________________
5. ____________________

Person 2: ____________________

1. ____________________
2. ____________________
3. ____________________
4. ____________________
5. ____________________

Person 3: ____________________

1. ____________________
2. ____________________
3. ____________________
4. ____________________
5. ____________________

Person 4: ____________________

1. ____

2. ____

3. ____

4. ____

5. ____

Person 5: ____________________

1. ____

2. ____

3. ____

4. ____

5. ____

Claim those for yourself; these are aspects of yourself that you want to cultivate and actualize in yourself. Keep them in mind as you figure out ways to live them more fully.

Then, research avenues to develop and use them, such as jobs and activities that would give you an opportunity to express the qualities you identified.

Starting Your Own Business

Some people are simply more comfortable being their own bosses. They prefer the road less traveled. Appealing as this might sound, it isn't necessarily the easiest route to follow. When you factor in the financial realities—no more steady paycheck or paid vacations, the expense of health insurance, and the loss of your 401(k)—it comes down to this: You'd better really want it.

Having your own business is often a dream of escape. But regardless of whether you're a disgruntled corporate refugee, a college dropout, or a B-school graduate, you'd better have a destination before you sign up for the "pioneer track." After all, to be your own boss is to determine your own fate.

To paraphrase Eileen Ford, who built one of the most successful modeling agencies in the world: When you own your own business, success and satisfaction don't come from the tooth fairy or a magical white knight. You have to work like crazy to succeed. To stay motivated under those conditions, it helps if you've followed your heart, says Richie Melman, founder of Chicago-based Lettuce Entertain You, which owns and runs more than 30 successful restaurants. If you don't do what you love and know best, he says, you won't be able to compete with people who do love their businesses.

But what if your heart is parched with fear, anger, and self-doubt, perhaps because of a recent job loss? Many a corporate empire has been built on the back of an individual's anger and frustration. Dr. Edward Land's frustration with Kodak's unwillingness to back his dream of manufacturing an instant camera turned into the foundation for a photographic empire called Polaroid. For *Playboy* founder Hugh Hefner, the decision to "go solo" was a direct response to a rebuff. While working at *Esquire,* Hefner asked his boss for a $5 raise and got turned down. He quit to make his fortune where his contribution would be more appreciated.

Although anger can fuel healthy competitive instincts, it can also be self-destructive. However temporarily liberating they might be, rage and revenge motives aren't a good foundation for long-term career satisfaction. You need a deeper commitment to sustain you for long-term success.

Lloyd Shefsky, a Chicago attorney and author of *Entrepreneurs Are Made, Not Born* (1994, McGraw-Hill), thinks that many entrepreneurs make the mistake of viewing their businesses like newborn children. He says the more appropriate metaphor is that of a marriage or a partnership, not a parent-child relationship.

From Cavorter to Tycoon

We can all take a lesson from Neil Balter, who successfully channeled his adolescent rage (and energies) into a small corporate empire. Balter caught the entrepreneurial bug when he was a teenager, almost by default.

Balter's parents kicked him out of the house at age 17 for having a bad attitude. In teenage terms, that means he was out "cavorting" until all hours of the night, sleeping late, skipping school, and barely passing his classes. This hardly sounds like the background of an ambitious executive who'd become a millionaire before he was 30 years old. But that's exactly what happened.

Forced out on his own, Balter had to find a way to make a living. An excellent carpenter, he put his talents to use converting his neighbors' messy closets into custom-built bastions of organization. Working from the back of his van, he ended up grossing $60,000 in his first year of business. Twelve years later, he sold his highly successful California Closet Co. to Williams-Sonoma Inc. for $12 million.

It helped Balter tremendously that he had a mentor: a "believer" in the form of a friend's dad who fronted him the $1,000 and van he needed to get started in exchange for a piece of the action. A few years later, Balter's "fairy godfather" sold his share back to Neil and his dad—with whom he made amends—for $20,000. It was sorely needed financial and emotional support. Like many new ventures, Balter was pitifully undercapitalized and highly dependent on "sweat equity." Along the way, he met up with many doomsayers, accountants and lawyers who were convinced that no 17-year-old kid could make the concept work, no matter how great his carpentry skills might be. (Let's face it: There are lots of carpenters who never become millionaires.) But Balter had that odd combination of ambition, drive, and naïveté that sometimes outsparkles the more judicious voices of conventional wisdom.

The Benefits of Preparation

Nonetheless, there's something to be said for preparation. While Balter can argue for the "school of hard knocks" over traditional education, most of today's more successful entrepreneurs are formally educated. In today's more sophisticated economy, it is not unusual for successful entrepreneurs to hold college and even graduate degrees in business or technical specialties.

Tim Prince typifies this sort of entrepreneur. Prince started out, though, as a traditional corporate ladder-climber. Right after college, he joined Airmax, a transportation-management company in Chicago. It was an exciting place for Prince to work because it was growing quickly. In five years, he worked his way up the ranks from customer service to marketing to sales management. Along the way, he was inspired by the vision and leadership of Ken Ryan, his boss and mentor there. It was from him that he caught the entrepreneurial bug. Soon, Prince decided to try his own hand at business ownership.

At 28 years old, though, Prince didn't feel he had enough confidence, skill, or credibility to go it entirely alone. Having been well mentored, he really appreciated the value of such a partnership. It seemed to him that buying a franchise might be a good way to test his entrepreneurial wings. After researching the marketplace, he decided on ServiceMaster because the systems and mentors were already in place.

Prince liked ServiceMaster's policy of teaming new franchisees up with more experienced owners to help them through those rocky first years. He knows that, as a newcomer to business ownership, he's bound to make mistakes. But to him that's the price of the experience—the cost of trying something new.

"This is my MBA," he says. "I'm really going to learn how to run and grow a business." Now that he's just getting started, he finds the process both scary and exhilarating. "Airmax taught me that you can't be afraid of change," says Prince. "If you're afraid to change, you won't make the moves you need to make to keep growing."

Do You Have What It Takes to Become an Entrepreneur?

Like many of the entrepreneurial hopefuls that I counsel, I always knew that I wanted to be self-employed. But until I chanced on the field of psychology, I never knew what kind of business I wanted to own. After more than 12 years of career counseling, I've learned that most new business ideas come from an in-depth knowledge of an industry or field, a meaningful life experience, or a hobby or other extracurricular activity.

Most self-employed consultants fall into the first category. If you've been working in one industry for a decade or more, consulting might seem like a natural outlet for your expertise. In fact, it's become the siren song of the decade for many early retirees, job hunters, and dissatisfied executives. But it's not a panacea for career unhappiness. Building a consulting business takes more than hanging out a shingle and waiting for business to come to you. Besides industry expertise, you also need self-confidence, a market for your services, a financial cushion, some salesmanship...and time. It's not an easy ride; you'll have to get in the boat and row to your destination.

New York City career counselor Anita Lands believes that many people have unrealistic expectations about what it means to be self-employed. "They're operating more out of fantasy than reality and may be in for a rude awakening," she says. "You have to be a very self-motivated person to make it work. If you don't generate activity, nothing will move. It's all up to you."

Phyllis Edelen admits she underestimated the amount of marketing time and skill it takes to build a successful business. Although she's a dynamic trainer with outstanding organizational skills, sales and marketing aren't her idea of a good time. When Edelen formed her own human-resources consulting firm in Gary, Indiana, she didn't expect to return to a more structured environment later. But circumstances changed and so did she.

For starters, she got married. As a newlywed, Edelen felt a need to curtail her extensive travel schedule so that she could spend more time with her husband. This definitely put a crimp in her work life. The harsh truth is this: If you want to do interesting and challenging work, you have to be willing to travel to where that work is. Otherwise, you can stagnate. Dreaming of a no-travel schedule, Edelen jumped at an opportunity to help manage an AT&T outplacement center in Chicago. Technically, she was still a consultant on an account, but it would be hard to tell her from a regular staffer. Indeed, for any consultant who craves variety, challenge, and freedom of movement, it wouldn't be an appealing solution. Translated into real-life terms, Edelen worked 9 a.m. to 5 p.m., four or five days a week, for 2½ years. When that assignment ended, she took a short break before accepting another 9-to-5 position managing Kraft's downstate-Illinois career-transition center.

"I may be self-employed," says Edelen, "but in my case, the only difference between self-employment and a J.O.B. is the cost of health insurance and a 401(k) plan." She is not alone. Many of her former colleagues have made similar decisions. In an intensely competitive market, consultants who lack marketing ambition are finding it increasingly difficult to compete for more desirable assignments with their more extroverted counterparts.

That said, there's no mandate that only highly extroverted sales types are cut out for self-employment. Although gregariousness certainly helps, you can overcome that lack by hiring people who complement you and offset your limitations.

Consider Wheaton, Illinois, financial planner Peggy Tracy. She lives the independent consultant's dream—thanks, in part, to the assistance of Julia Schopick, an Oak Park, Illinois, public-relations professional who specializes in promoting doctors, lawyers, accountants, and other professionals.

Tracy went independent after leaving her job as assistant accounting manager for a financial services company. She wanted to concentrate on doing the work rather than getting it, so she hired Schopick to help promote her business and carve out a niche where her services would be welcome. The result: Clients seek her out and she's created a very profitable business. Their collaboration is a textbook example of how two consulting businesses can profit by working together.

Certainly, the ideal may be to spend a decade developing expertise and influence within a specific industry before launching a business. However, when it comes to entrepreneurialism, exceptions make the rules. If all would-be owners took the time to work their way up the corporate ladder before carefully planning and starting their own firms, the U.S. economy would boast far fewer entrepreneurial success stories.

Joe Mansueto had a love of investing and an unusual—almost cultish—fascination with mutual funds. His belief in them became the foundation for a Chicago publishing firm that covers mutual funds the way newspapers cover sports. Entrepreneurs are, by nature, builders and creators—not just of products and services, but also of communities. They're mavericks determined to mold the world to suit their needs and dreams. In many ways, Mansueto is the classic entrepreneur. Yes, he had some of those innate childhood leanings. When he was nine years old, he decided to sell crickets to the neighbors as garden accessories. He ordered 1,000 to get started. It turned out to be his first entrepreneurial failure: The crickets died.

Almost from the beginning, he had a great eye for a value. As a sixth grader, he was a ham radio buff. This hobby netted him his first real taste of financial success when he bought a vintage radio for $100 and sold it two weeks later for $300. But he admits that the community mattered more to him than the money. The camaraderie he shared with other ham-radio fanatics has stayed with him as a happy memory.

As an adult, when it came time to get a "real job," he sought one that would suit his casual lifestyle, intellectual curiosity, and sense of community. He founded Morningstar to create it. As the company grew, his role was constantly changing. Businesses, like people, have different developmental stages and need different types of leaders at different times in their histories. For him, that is part of the challenge.

Creating Your Own Community

Manseuto enjoys building a community that reflects his values and vision. Although many entrepreneurs are driven by a desire to make money, others are driven by a need to create community, reminiscent of this T.S. Eliot quote:

> *When the stranger says: "What is the meaning of this city? Do you huddle together because you love one another?" What will you answer? "We all dwell together to make money from each other," or "This is a community"?*

That's the wonderful thing about deciding to become an entrepreneur. If you don't like the people you work with and for, you can change those dynamics by selecting yourself to be your own boss and hiring people you respect and admire to work for you. Would you call that self-empowerment or self-employment?

Acting Self-Employed

Perhaps *your* ambitions don't include a desire to head up an incredibly high-growth company, but you'd like a little more money and a lot more freedom. If so, Northbrook, Illinois, human resources consultant Lou Ella Jackson advises bringing more of a self-employed attitude to your current career. In practical employment terms, that means greater self-reliance and better collaborative partnerships.

Rube Lemarque, a retired AT&T sales and marketing manager, might have carried that concept to the extreme. Lemarque is now a freelance professor who keeps six packed briefcases in the office of his

Arlington Heights, Illinois, home. The briefcases contain materials and paperwork for the business courses he teaches at three different Illinois colleges. Like Paladin of *Have Gun, Will Travel,* you need only call Lemarque and he'll bring his knowledge to you.

His new role requires Herculean organizational skills and an extraordinary facility for remembering where he's supposed to be when and what he's supposed to be teaching to whom. Still, he's loving every minute of his new work style. Because his ultimate goal is to land one full-time instructorship at a college, his current itinerary is a wonderful opportunity to gain experience with a variety of different schools and students to see what fits him best.

As part of a new cadre of workers who are temporarily self-employed, this 50+ executive is taking a very aggressive stance toward his vocational future. This is the new advice that career experts everywhere are touting. If you want to be successful and happy, manage your career as if it were a company of one. Because no matter whom you work for, your career is your business. Even if you never get to be the official Big Kahuna, you're still the CEO of your own life.

We, Inc.: Working with Others or Starting Your Own Business Thought-Starter Worksheet

1. How do you get along with your boss?

____

____

2. What can you do to improve that relationship?

____

____

____

(continues)

(continued)

3. Have you ever considered a lateral move?

____

4. Would you like to be your own boss?

Yes

5. What kind of business would you like to have?

Gallery owner/landlord

____

____

6. Do your skills and experience lend themselves to any particular options?

ART / therapy / education

____

____

7. Would you describe yourself as a risk-taker?

NO

8. What kind of risk do you feel most comfortable taking?

ones that don't lead to rejection

____

9. Does this have any implications for your future as an entrepreneur?

____

____

____

10. Do you see yourself as someone with a lot of energy and persistence?

~~no~~ / sometimes

11. Are you good at creative problem-solving?

Yes

12. How do you normally deal with failure?

take it bad, then learn from it

13. Do you often motivate other people?

sometimes

14. Of the examples cited in this chapter, who did you admire the most? Why?

15. In the past, how much responsibility have you taken for your own career development?

a lot

16. Can you picture any ways you can take more responsibility?

APPENDIX

Your Career Happiness Plan

You get the adventure you are ready for.

—Joseph Campbell

This set of worksheets is like a performance appraisal. You can use it to set developmental goals or improve your performance. But its real purpose is to help you increase your overall career satisfaction. You can retake it again in a few months or a year to see how far you've progressed toward becoming a happier, more fulfilled person.

Worksheet 1: Life Satisfaction Indicator

On a scale from 1 to 5 (5 = completely satisfied, 3 = so-so, and 1 = not at all), how satisfied are you with your life?

5 4 3 2 1

Now, rank each of the following areas of your Life Satisfaction Indicator individually:

Career satisfaction	5	4	3	2	1
Job satisfaction	5	4	3	2	1
Spouse/partner	5	4	3	2	1
Health	5	4	3	2	1
Friends	5	4	3	2	1
Religious involvement	5	4	3	2	1
Personal development	5	4	3	2	1
Professional development	5	4	3	2	1

Which areas require your most concentrated effort?

Job satisfaction/friendship

Worksheet 2: Taking Your Career Satisfaction Temperature

With "Icy Cold" being worst and "Hot" being best, how satisfied are you right now with the following aspects of your work?

Advancement/level of achievement	Icy Cold	Cool	Lukewarm	Hot
Autonomy (ability to work independently)	Icy Cold	Cool	Lukewarm	Hot
Challenge	Icy Cold	Cool	Lukewarm	Hot
Collegiality	Icy Cold	Cool	Lukewarm	Hot
Contribution	Icy Cold	Cool	Lukewarm	Hot
Control over income	Icy Cold	Cool	Lukewarm	Hot
Control over time	Icy Cold	Cool	Lukewarm	Hot
Control over workload	Icy Cold	Cool	Lukewarm	Hot
Creative challenge	Icy Cold	Cool	Lukewarm	Hot
Desire to serve	Icy Cold	Cool	Lukewarm	Hot
Development of potential	Icy Cold	Cool	Lukewarm	Hot
Education/training	Icy Cold	Cool	Lukewarm	Hot
Growth	Icy Cold	Cool	Lukewarm	Hot
Intellectual stimulation	Icy Cold	Cool	Lukewarm	Hot
Job security	Icy Cold	Cool	Lukewarm	Hot
Lifestyle considerations	Icy Cold	Cool	Lukewarm	Hot
Meaningfulness	Icy Cold	Cool	Lukewarm	Hot
Mentoring	Icy Cold	Cool	Lukewarm	Hot
Money	Icy Cold	Cool	Lukewarm	Hot
Organizational affiliation	Icy Cold	Cool	Lukewarm	Hot
Power	Icy Cold	Cool	Lukewarm	Hot
Personal productivity	Icy Cold	Cool	Lukewarm	Hot
Recognition and respect	Icy Cold	Cool	Lukewarm	Hot
Sense of mastery	Icy Cold	Cool	Lukewarm	Hot

(continues)

(continued)

Status/prestige	Icy Cold	Cool	Lukewarm	Hot
Success	Icy Cold	Cool	Lukewarm	Hot
Technical competence	Icy Cold	Cool	Lukewarm	Hot
Wealth	Icy Cold	Cool	Lukewarm	Hot

Worksheet 3: A Second Reading

List the factors you indicated as "Icy Cold" or "Cool" in worksheet 2. Then indicate the importance of each factor to your overall career satisfaction.

	Very Important	Somewhat Important	Not Important
1.	Autonomy → find it elsewhere		
2.	Control of time → accept		
3.		Education → do it myself	
4.			Mentoring
5.		affiliation → make effort	
6.		Power → find it elsewhere	
7.		Status → fine	
8.		Wealth → fine	
9.			
10.			

Worksheet 4: Action Alert

When something is very important to you, yet you receive no pleasure or satisfaction in that area, you must develop a plan to get that particular need, value, or desire met. For the factors you listed as "very important" or "somewhat important" in worksheet 3, brainstorm about steps you can take to improve your satisfaction with them. Write down your ideas in the space provided here. If you have trouble with this, review the chapter or chapters that are most relevant to your particular concerns.

____

____

____

____

____

____

Worksheet 5: Accomplishment Profile

Feeling good about your accomplishments is an important source of career satisfaction. To help you do that, use the space provided to write about five (or more) things you've achieved in your career or personal life that make you feel proud and satisfied.

Story 1:

Workable relationship w/ boss

Story 2:

Improving written & verbal french

Story 3:

starting several pilot projects

Story 4:

learning embroidery

Story 5:

learning to be real/friendlier

Do you see any patterns or themes in these stories? Has this exercise given you some insight on which skills you most enjoy using or how you like to work? If so, document them here.

self-improvement, growth

Worksheet 6: Job Satisfaction Profile

Write down the last 10 jobs you've held (either with different employers or within the same company). If you haven't had 10 jobs, list as many as you can. Then, rank each position according to your level of enjoyment or satisfaction with it. The one you enjoyed most will be 1, the next will be 2, and so on. Finally, indicate why you found these jobs enjoyable.

	Job	Ranking	Reasons
1.	Ed par l'art	2	diverse/challenging
	art teacher CREP	4	diverse pop/autonomy
2.	art teacher/Saidye	3	Fun/autonomy
3.	art therapist/blind kids	1	challenging/autonomou[s]
4.	art therapist/retarded adults	5	in my field/strange vib with boss
5.	clerk/physio	7	boring
6.	clerk/hospital	6	tought me professionalism, empathy
7.	sales	8	sucked
8.			
9.			
10.			

Worksheet 7: Family Ties

We all inherit a work heritage from our families that can consciously or unconsciously influence our choices and/or level of satisfaction. It might help you now to remember that heritage and get back in touch with some of your early influences. To do that, think as far back in time as you need to, to recall your relationships with your parents, grandparents, and siblings. Ask yourself, "What did they want from me, anyway?":

My Dad wanted me to...

____

____

____

My Mom wanted me to...

____

____

____

My brother __________ wanted me to...

____

____

____

My sister __________ wanted me to...

____

____

____

(continues)

(continued)

My grandfather wanted me to...

____

____

____

My grandmother wanted me to...

____

____

____

Now, draw up a composite picture of what the "perfect child" would look like based on the roster of family expectations you've just compiled:

Worksheet 8: The Phantom of the Family

Most families have an overidealized hero. Usually, this is someone who hasn't been around to correct that impression. In my family, my grandfather has always been described as an extremely gentle, highly principled, intelligent, all-loving man. Because he died when I was only six years old, it's hard to know how much truth there is to that portrait. But I do know that it has influenced my family's values and career choices.

What about your family icon? Who was the carrier of the family values? How did that person influence your choices and decisions, either directly or indirectly?

Father → do something creative
→ $ = freedom!
→ Family isn't a priority

Worksheet 9: The Wizard Within

In *The Wizard of Oz,* the main characters all longed for something they felt they really needed to be happy. The Scarecrow needed brains, the Tin Woodsman needed a heart, the Lion needed courage, and Dorothy needed a way to return home. What about yourself? In the following list, put a check next to the traits you need to cultivate to become more satisfied:

_____ Like the Scarecrow, I need more experience in the world and a chance to use and develop my knowledge and skill.

_____ Like the Tin Woodsman, I need to recover from my traumas so that I can recapture my heart and passion.

__✓__ Like the Lion, I need to learn bravery and courage—to take more chances.

__✓__ Like Dorothy, I need to learn how to recognize and use the resources that are available to me. I need more confidence in my abilities and an education in the ways of the world.

Worksheet 10: Facing Your Fears

Sometimes people back into choices because they anticipate (and fear) the consequences of making a choice. Look at the following list to identify and evaluate your personal fear factors.

	Terrified	**Somewhat Scared**	**A Little Scared**	**I Can Handle It**
1. How would you feel if you lost your job?	✓			
2. Do you worry that you're unmarketable because of your skills, education, or age?			✓	
3. How do you feel about your ability to support yourself if you don't have a job?			✓	
4. How does the thought of job hunting make you feel?			✓	
5. Do you worry that you'll fail?			✓	
6. Are you worried that people you care about will be disappointed or abandon you if you fail?				✓
7. Do you ever fear success?			✓	
8. Have you ever been scared that your success might make other people envious?			✓	
9. How do you feel about retirement?				✓

(continues)

(continued)

	Terrified	Somewhat Scared	A Little Scared	I Can Handle It
10. Do you worry that you don't have enough money to retire?				
11. Does inactivity scare you?				
12. Do you often worry that people will think you're naïve?				
13. How do you feel about authority?				
14. Do you ever worry that you'll never find a job you like?				
15. Are you afraid of getting trapped in a bad situation?				
16. How do you feel when you stand up for your rights and beliefs?				
17. What's your attitude toward confrontation?				
18. How do you feel about letting other people down?				
19. Do you worry that you'll never "find yourself" or use your full potential?				
20. Are you afraid to hope for too much?				

Worksheet 11: Judgment Day

Summarize your top 10 worst career-related fears from worksheet 10:

To overcome

1. fear of losing my job → be realistic
2. trapped in bad sit → take risk
3. won't find good job → have faith
4. fear of confront → baby steps
5.
6.
7.
8.
9.
10.

Are there any practical, concrete steps you can take that will make you feel more confident about the challenges you must tackle to build a more satisfying work life? For example, to fight the fear of job hunting, you can read job search books, prepare a great resume, work with a counselor, and practice interviewing. Or, if you're afraid you aren't marketable, you might read about employment trends and opportunities, look for projects in your company that will allow you to build valuable skills and experience, sign up for training courses in hot new areas, and so on.

(continues)

(continued)

Now, you try it:

Fear: ____

Steps to Overcome Fear **Timetable**

1. ____

2. ____

3. ____

4. ____

5. ____

Fear: ____

Steps to Overcome Fear **Timetable**

1. ____

2. ____

3. ____

4. ____

5. ____

Fear: ______________________________

Steps to Overcome Fear **Timetable**

1. ______________________________

2. ______________________________

3. ______________________________

4. ______________________________

5. ______________________________

Worksheet 12: A Second Opinion

If your "fear factors" in worksheet 11 are too high, you need to think more aggressively about your situation and set some developmental goals to strengthen your confidence. The following checklist should help you get started.

To be less fearful and anxious, I need to:

1. Improve my skills. ______
2. Develop more confidence in my abilities. __✓__
3. Develop my interests more. __✓__
4. Get involved in more social or community activities. __✓__
5. Communicate my needs better to family and friends. __✓__
6. Upgrade my education. ______
7. Expand my network. __✓__
8. Trust my instincts more. ______
9. Stand up for my rights and beliefs. __✓__
10. Find a suitable mentor. ______
11. Stop procrastinating. ______
12. Know more about the job market. __✓__
13. Get professional assistance. ______
14. Improve my job-hunting skills. __✓__

15. Learn to think more positively. ✓

16. Ask for help when I need it. ✓

17. Be less critical of others. ✓

18. Be less critical of myself. ✓

19. Stop being a victim and take more responsibility for my own happiness. ✓

Of the things you need to do to improve your frame of mind (and your situation), which ones are you willing to start working on right now?

Dev confidence

Dev interests

Involved in community

think positive

less critical

Worksheet 13: Development Planning

For each area of weakness in worksheet 12 that you said you'd work on immediately, set a developmental goal and create a plan to get there.

Example

Goal: Develop my interests more.

Action Plan	**Date**
1. Go to the bookstore and consider my browsing habits. What topics call out to me?	Oct. 15
2. Go to a music store. Buy or listen to something completely new and different and keep an open mind about liking it.	Oct. 17
3. Take an interest test to clarify my interests.	Nov. 1
4. Read the newspaper's events calendar and commit to attending one totally new activity.	Nov. 10
5. Talk to friends and acquaintances about their hobbies, activities, and interests.	Ongoing, start now

Now, it's your turn:

Goal: ______________________________

Action Plan	**Date**
1. ______________________________	
2. ______________________________	
3. ______________________________	

4. ______________________________

5. ______________________________

Goal: ______________________

Action Plan **Date**

1. ______________________________

2. ______________________________

3. ______________________________

4. ______________________________

5. ______________________________

Worksheet 14: Your Spiritual Deficits

The following exercise will help you identify "what's missing" from your spiritual work life. Place a check mark next to the statements that best apply to you.

I need:

1. More emotional connection with my work. ✓
2. To work more closely with people who share my values and beliefs. ______
3. A chance to develop and use my creativity. ✓
4. More freedom. ✓
5. More balance.
6. To feel that my work makes more of a contribution to society. ______
7. To feel a greater sense of purpose. ______
8. More interesting work. ______
9. More challenging work. ✓
10. A career, not a job. ______

Worksheet 15: Action Alert

1. Write down your most urgent need from those you articulated in worksheet 14.

Freedom

2. Is there anything you can do to begin fulfilling that need? If so, what's a reasonable first step?

Continuing to be my own boss

3. Write down a reasonable timetable for accomplishing that first step.

5 to 10 years

4. Do any other people (spouse, parent, boss) need to know your goal and timetable? If so, how do you plan to approach them?

Worksheet 16: Harnessing Your Brilliance

1. Identify your most unique talent, gift, or skill (for example, I can really read people; I'm a brilliant sailor; I'm a master negotiator).

organization/self-motivation

2. Script a scenario in which you use your greatest gift or talent productively in the job market.

3. Now, let your imagination run wild. Brainstorm all the ways you could use your talent or gift in the work world if you let your brilliance run wild. Be specific. Where would you work? Who would you work with? What would you do?

Gallery owner

4. What practical constraints prevent you from developing and applying your talents?

5. If someone (or something) other than you is holding you back or down, is your commitment to that person or activity more important than your own growth? If so, why?

6. Ten years from now, how do you think you'll feel about yourself if you don't develop your talents or meet your potential?

7. Is that emotional reality acceptable to you?

(continues)

(continued)

8. Think carefully: If you could fully develop your potential, how do you think it would make you feel? (Check as many of the following as you like.)

___✓___	happy	___✓___	excited
______	content	______	grateful
___✓___	scared	___✓___	insecure
______	worried	______	betrayed
______	sad	______	overwhelmed
______	other		

9. Do any of those feelings account for your inaction? If so, how?

____

____

____

____

10. Write an ending to your own story in which you use your talents happily ever after.

____

____

____

____

INDEX

H

I

J–K

L

R

S